Women in
Church
and
Society

Women in Church and Society

A Historical and Theological Inquiry

GEORGIA HARKNESS

Nashville ABINGDON PRESS New York

WOMEN IN CHURCH AND SOCIETY

Copyright © 1972 by Abingdon Press

ISBN 0-687-45965-6

Library of Congress Catalog Card Number: 76-172809

SET UP, PRINTED, AND BOUND BY THE
PARTHENON PRESS, AT NASHVILLE,
TENNESSEE, UNITED STATES OF AMERICA

Preface

Why another book on women, when in recent years books and articles on the subject have been pouring from the presses? Has not everything been said that should be said on the subject? There is a threefold reason why I have undertaken this study.

My first concern is the fact that, in spite of much publicity on the Women's Liberation Front, not much has been done to change the conditions which have produced it. Employed women, however well prepared, continue to receive only about sixty cents to the male dollar and to be employed for the most part in subordinate or routine positions without hope of advancement to important decision-making posts. Women often rise in salary only to the point where a man starts, and in the professions, as in industry, highly trained and capable women serve mainly in the "house-keeping" jobs requiring minor skills.

After fifty years of woman suffrage, there are very few women in government—one woman in the Senate with 99 men, 12 in the House of Representatives with 423 men. In State legislatures and even in most local governments, women have a very minor place. To have the vote has by no means assured to women either economic or political equality of opportunity.

In the churches the situation is comparable, but in some respects worse. Women comprise well over half the membership of churches; yet the number chosen to

47907

represent the churches in governing denominational or ecumenical bodies is a small fraction of the male representation. In spite of recent steps taken in several major Protestant denominations to open ordination to women, the congregations willing to accept a woman minister, even at a meager salary for which a man cannot be had, are few in number. Women are admitted readily to most of the Protestant seminaries, but upon graduation neither preaching nor teaching positions, except in rare instances, are open to them. A generation ago many women were employed as directors of Christian education, but now a male minister of education is increasingly preferred.

Such facts need to be recognized, and consciences aroused thereby to correct injustices. Because the issues in both the churches and the larger society are closely intertwined, I have chosen to present them together but with a special emphasis from the angle of the churches.

A second concern which has prompted this writing is that much of the Women's Liberation literature which has appeared has a secular base. This finds justification from the fact that every writer must speak to the world from his or her own position in it. Since my position during a long professional career has been centered in the church and in an attempt to interpret the Christian gospel, it is natural that I should speak from this point of view while others do so from differing angles.

The reader will find here and there some reflections of personal experiences as I have lived through these years in my denomination (the Methodist) and in the ecumenical movement. However, the book is not intended to be mainly autobiographical, and I hope it is written without animus, for I have been extraordinarily well treated in the churches. But, to quote Paul, "my heart's desire and prayer to God" is that the churches may become alerted to the need and the possibilities of a greater place for women's leadership in many fields. Should this come about, there could be a great enlargement of the services of women both to the churches and through them to society as a whole.

A third concern which has determined the scope of the book is the need to combine the historical background of the problem with a theological appraisal of it. As far as I know, this has not been done elsewhere in this manner. A linkage of history with theology is helpful in giving perspective on any social issue, but is especially necessary in this field.

Accordingly, the book will fall into two parts, of which the first is historical. To grasp the sweep of history is essential to understanding conditions and directing procedures in the present, for in this as in other matters, "what is past is prologue." We must look at some evidences of women's agelong subjection to men, but also at such steps as have been taken toward greater equality and wider opportunities. Since most of these developments have come about in the nineteenth and twentieth centuries, a considerable part of the study will center in this period.

The second part of the book is biblical and theological. It is familiar knowledge that according to the second chapter of Genesis, woman was made from Adam's rib to be man's helper, and that Paul said some things not very favorable to the status of women. Everybody knows also, or should know, that the Christian gospel stands for the equality of all persons before God. These matters, and what to do with their apparent contradiction, have been taken up in a number of other books on women in the church. However, I have found little

7

that attempts to give a comprehensive theological study of these and other related issues. But unless we build from firm theological foundations, how shall we find the right guidelines?

It is with the hope that this book may provide some such guidelines, and with them a stimulus to greater justice in a vital human relation, that these pages are presented. The book aims to be both descriptive and constructive, both historical and theological. To what extent these aims are achieved must be the reader's decision.

GEORGIA HARKNESS

Contents

I The next revolution

This is a book about women—women in the churches, but other women as well, for there is no clear dividing line. The women's movement is the newest among the many of our time. Yet in another sense it is not new, for its occasional manifestations and the conditions which produce them go back to the beginnings of human history.

The women's movement is more than a struggle for "women's rights," though it contains this element. It is essentially a struggle for the recognition of women as persons of equal worth and status with men, and with equal opportunities according to their talents, training, and various forms of ability. In its more authentic forms it does not deny or disparage the fact of biological differences between the sexes, with each needing the other, nor seek to repudiate the special obligations and duties which result from a woman's role in childbearing and motherhood. What it does protest is the too common assumption that these are a woman's only significant functions with subordination to men because of an innate inferiority in everything else.

I was somewhat startled a few years ago to hear it stated that the struggle for sex equality was likely to go on long after the battle for race equality had been won.[1] Upon consideration I believe this to be true. Sex discrimination--an ugly word but one that must be used—has deeper roots and more subtle manifestations than those based on race or color. The very fact that women appear to be held in high honor in modern civilized cultures tends to gloss over many facets of cultural subordination which women feel, but of which men are too prone not to be aware.

Thus it comes about that a new revolution is upon us, in the churches and all around us. To understand this it must be seen against the backdrop of the other revolutions of our time. Let us begin with a glance at some of these, reserving for the moment any estimate of the place of women in them. All are related, and each has contributed something to this new movement.

1. *Current revolutions*

No one at all acquainted with what is going on in the world needs to be told that this is an age of revolutionary ferment. Since the Second World War, a surge of nationalism in many formerly dependent areas has put an end to colonialism in most of the former empires. Within these new nations, which numerically make up the greater part of the United Nations, the demand for self-government and self-expression has spilled over from the political into numerous social and religious arenas. In any world assembly, whether it be of the United Nations and its subsidiary agencies or the World Council of Churches, the demand for equal rights and for forms of justice long denied comes through in clear and strong, even if sometimes in understandably strident, tones.[2]

To turn to a different but related revolution, disturbance on American campuses is no isolated phenomenon. There is a worldwide student revolt which demands both a voice in the governing of educational institutions and an abrupt break with alignment with any institution, commercial, financial, or governmental, which supports war-making, racial injustice, or economic oppression. Despite demands and modes of demanding which often seem unreasonable to their elders, the interest of today's student in social action and the world he lives in far exceeds that of earlier student generations and often outruns his interest in academic pursuits. Yet regarding the latter also he insists on having a say. To the discomfiture of some faculty members while others welcome it, the old familiar modes of lecturing, examining, and grading on the basis of the teacher's pabulum no longer work; the students insist on saying both *what* and *how* they shall be taught.

In America we are obviously in the midst of a large-scale revolution in civil rights. This came to a head and for a time seemed to be largely achieved in the passage of the Civil Rights Act of 1964 and the Voting Rights Act of 1965. However, it soon became evident that, important as these steps were, they no more solved the basic problems of civil rights than did the historic decision of the Supreme Court in 1954 when it called for the racial integration of the public schools. This issue along with related ones in matters of housing, employment, penology and justice in the courts is with us in full force.

The Black Power movement with its many ramifications has emerged, too large and controversial an issue to be characterized in any detail in this brief survey. However, its central issue is the resolve of the black man to slough off the image of inferiority in which he has long been held, not only by others but by himself, and gain a new sense of his identity and dignity as a person. This lies at the base of what white persons find so hard

15

to understand—a trend toward black separatism rather than the goal of the integration of the races.[3] Less conspicuously but with a determination that at least approximates a revolution, other ethnic minority groups are asserting that they too have rights that have long been denied, and they will no longer passively tolerate this situation.

In such encounters, whether between the young and their elders or between the races, violence with counter-violence erupts all too frequently. It is often overlooked that this violence is far less in its proportions than the amount of friendly interchange and adjustment among those of differing backgrounds in school, business, and community. It naturally seems greater because when it occurs it is news—startling news. Yet it is serious enough to constitute a deep cleavage in our culture, a cleavage which has long been latent but is now overt.

In the field of economics, collective bargaining and the right of labor to organize—much in the forefront of revolutionary demands in the early part of the twentieth century—were for the most part won a generation ago. It is revealing to compare the original Social Creed of the Methodist Church, formulated in 1908, with the generally accepted principles of today. In that era the twelve-hour day and the seven-day week were not unusual. Labor unions were few and the formation of each new union strongly opposed by most employers. Hence there was something revolutionary about such statements as these:

The Methodist Episcopal Church stands:—

For the principle of conciliation and arbitration in industrial dissensions. . . .

For the suppression of the "sweating system." . . .

For the gradual and reasonable reduction of the hours of labor to the lowest practical point, with work for all. . . .

For a release from employment one day in seven. . . .⁴

Great advances have been made within this century toward protection of the rights of the employed, such advances that "the working poor" if they can find employment are now often very well off through the power of the unions, and the consumer has to pay fantastic prices for the services of a carpenter or plumber. Yet shocking poverty remains in more than a few areas of American life. Agricultural labor, especially "stoop labor," the migrants, the dwellers in Appalachian shacks, and the urban poor living in rat and roach infested ghettos have yet to attain the right to live in conditions of health, dignity, and reasonable comfort. The economic revolution continues and is likely to for a long time.

Overshadowing and permeating all other revolutionary protests in the American scene is the war in Southeast Asia. The students and other young people of the country, if not unanimous in their demand that the war and all its adjuncts be ended, are so largely of this opinion that repeated demonstrations are inevitable. Their elders are divided between a traditional anticommunism and "support the government" position on the one hand, and on the other, agreement with the young that the present war is so unjust and immoral that its continuance cannot be justified. The result is a polarization which divides the country more deeply than at any time since the Civil War, and if exception be made of the fratricidal bloodshed of the 1861-65 period, the country is probably more deeply divided than at any time since the Republic was founded.

The effects of this division affect American life in

17

many aspects of its existence. The widespread feeling that money is lavishly being poured down the drain in Vietnam which could and should be used for much-needed domestic programs steps up all the other forms of revolution that have been noted. While as in the past the majority would doubtless support a war in defense of this country, the giving up of precious American lives year after year in a country that most Americans never heard of until the war started, and in support of a dictatorial foreign government that may not merit such support, generates much unrest. In addition to such causes of distrust of our government's policies, the feeling that Congress is being bypassed by the waging of an undeclared war raises a vital Constitutional question. Everybody wants to see the war ended or says he does—on that there is no expressed disagreement. But there is deep disagreement as to when and how and under what terms to end it, and deep dissension over the protests and demonstrations in regard to it. All this amounts to a full-scale revolution which is likely to outlast the ending of the war, whenever and however that may come about.

Further confusion is added to all these factors by the new morality and the revolution in codes of conduct, which centers in no small measure in the abolition of such codes. In part this is a theoretical approach, which under the aegis of "situation ethics" professes to cling to love as an all-encompassing norm, but actually gives little guidance and is almost if not wholly antinomian and amorphous in its stance. Were this limited to the ethical theorists, it might not be so revolutionary, for those whose names are most often connected with it live very normal lives which reflect the traditional virtues.[5] But taken over by the immature who have built up no sustaining social disciplines for their behavior, it means "doing one's own thing," often interpreted as following one's own impulses, with little regard for the social consequences. When such a rejection of codes of conduct is accompanied by a rejection of "the Establishment" which is charged with having sanctioned them, confusion reigns and a cultural revolution is upon us.

Both puritanism and pietism have hard sledding in our time. This is not all loss. There were extremes in each of these outlooks which did not make for life at its fullest and best, or as we may well believe God would have it. Yet while there is gain in the break with the more extreme forms of each, the crux comes in the question of what is to replace them. The flouting of long-established social disciplines, particularly in the areas of sexual morality and cleanness of speech and life style, is part of the present cultural revolution but can hardly be regarded as a mark of progress.

To move to a less controversial area, there is a revolution in which progress seems undeniable, and in some respects it undergirds all the rest. This is the technological revolution, longer in the making but staggering in its achievements. To be sure, the recent concern over what it has done to the environment, thus enlisting a new and widespread interest in ecology which may bring about another revolution if it results in serious action, may be checked up against the technological revolution. Yet not even these consequences in the pollution of air and water and the marring or wasting of natural resources can blot out the significance of technological advances and the resulting changes in human life styles.

Since the dropping of the first atomic bomb in 1945 there has hung over mankind the awesome possibility of nuclear destruction. This is still with us, but it is less talked about now than two other forms taken by "the sword of Damocles"—overpopulation and the destruction of the environment. These are real dangers, and they ought to be seriously reckoned with and all available steps taken to avert them. Yet alarm ought not to overshadow satisfaction in the great achievements of this era. The twentieth century has seen so many new things brought into being that it is a marvelous time in which to be alive. Whether due to naturally good health or the achievements of medical science, there are probably thousands of persons now living who can remember seeing their first automobile or airplane, then taking their first journey in one of these conveyances, seeing their first movie in the days of the silent cinema, hearing their first message by radio, seeing and hearing their first television presentation. Our homes, our streets and highways, our places of business are full of the fruits of technology, and of the factories which produce and the stores which sell them.

The most conspicuous symbols of the technological era are probably the computer, nuclear fission, and the conquest of space, culminating in the moon landings. Yet so far has the technological revoltuion advanced that these are now very largely taken for granted. However, it is one of the principal determining factors in contemporary living. New nations eagerly seek its fruits, and with all its liabilities and the occasional yearning for "the good old days" when life was simpler, I know of no one who would want to surrender the benefits of the technological revolution if he could.

2. *The newest revolution*

It is not the purpose of this book to deal directly with any of these forms of revolution. They have been mentioned as background of the main theme of the book, and indirectly they impinge on all of us in one form or another. But what of the women's revolution, of which many for the first time have become aware? Women are participants in every one of these other revolutions, sometimes as victims whose plight calls for new steps toward justice, sometimes as victors over centuries of cultural subordination.

The long-suppressed women of the Third World are finding both voice and vote. In gatherings of the world church I have repeatedly been impressed with the caliber, both in speech and action, of the women representatives from formerly dependent and supposedly backward areas. The same may be said of those in U.N. agencies. Though most women are still the family burden-bearers, all but a few of the member nations of the U.N. now give their women the right to vote.[6] Miss Angie Brooks of Liberia became President of the United Nations General Assembly, as did Madame Pandit of India a number of years ago. While a woman President of the United States is probably still a long way off, both India and Israel have elected women as their Prime Ministers.

That women are eligible for higher education and professional training, with minds as good as those of men, is now an almost universally accepted situation. This does not mean that an equal number of women receive such education, even in affluent America, for where there is any lack of funds for higher education sons are usually given the preference over daughters.[7] Nor does it mean that women have equal opportunities for the professional use of their talents and training after they have graduated from these institutions of

21

learning. It is at this point that much of the protest of the women's movement centers.

Women are as conscious of deep-seated injustices because of racial prejudice as are men. An added problem emerges, however, from the fact that women of the Negro race can often secure employment while their men remain unemployed, and this precipitates a family crisis. If not so prominent in the protest movements toward racial equality, black women are there in the demonstrations demanding a new world for their children. Some women, like Marian Anderson, Coretta King, and Shirley Chisholm, the first black woman to be elected a member of Congress, have shown such remarkable ability and character that they are widely respected and admired.

In the field of economics, women both suffer the limitations and enjoy the fruits of the progress of labor toward greater power. But these fruits are seriously curtailed, not only by being limited to subordinate positions and pay in all but a few so-called "women's occupations," but by the special strains that fall upon the housewives and mothers of the poor. The entire area of economics is both so large and so important that I shall reserve further comment.

Women are, in general, more opposed to war than men, both to this war and to every other. It is a moot psychological point as to whether women are innately more tender, sympathetic, and compassionate than men, or if this is acquired through more intimate personal relations in motherhood and family love. Most women seem to be less aggressive and more sensitive to suffering than men, and it is certain that when they bear and rear the sons sent off to battle, they tend to feel that it must never happen again.

A generation ago, I think between the two World Wars, there was a popular song with the refrain, "I didn't raise my son to be a soldier." We no longer hear the song, but in such organizations as "Another Mother for Peace," or "Women Strike for Peace," or the older "Women's International League for Peace and Freedom," founded by Jane Addams in 1915, millions of women are expressing their longing for the end of the present carnage.

It is difficult to assess the place of women in the new morality. In my opinion they are probably not much better or worse than men in deviations from accepted codes, though the statistics seem to indicate somewhat less premarital intercourse among college women than men. In protests against "the Establishment," women in the new freedom of this era seem to protest as much as do the long-haired males. However, there are two important current differences. First, no woman wants to be used by a man simply for his pleasure and cast off at his pleasure, as in the Playboy philosophy. Second, more women than men favor the legalizing of abortions upon request, since many women feel that they ought to have the right to exercise control over their own bodies.

The technological revolution more than anything else has brought about both the current power of women and their frustration in its exercise. Women have vastly more leisure from their housework than formerly, though many feel trapped by its tasks which they do not find rewarding, either from the dullness and monotony of the tasks or from the fact that their families take such unpaid labor for granted without even the reward of appreciation. Women are trained for a multitude of forms of service in the world which their grandmothers and even their mothers never dreamed of, and they feel

23

the lack of self-fulfillment when their energy is limited to the household round of duties.[8]

Both for this reason and because in many families it takes two salaries to meet the family budget, large numbers of women are employed. Yet here there is much frustration which, beyond other considerations, is at the root of the women's movement. A woman may have a college education with one or more advanced degrees and still be able to find employment only in an unskilled or inferior position. Granted that she finds something more nearly to her taste or talents, it is seldom in an important executive or administrative position, and promotions to such are not forthcoming. The median wage for full-time women workers is 58.2 percent of that of men.[9] Often limited to part-time work either by the lack of child care centers or by the deliberate practice of hiring women on a part-time basis, they fail to receive such fringe benefits as health insurance, paid vacations, sick leave, profit sharing, retirement benefits, or tenure.

It is not surprising, therefore, that women in great numbers feel keenly the denial of equal opportunities for self-fulfillment, for service to society in areas in which they are competent, and for the compensation which their talents and training merit or which their personal and family needs require.

This newest revolution is less violent and less understood than any of the preceding ones. Only recently has much been heard about it, though the passage of the Equal Rights Amendment by the House of Representatives by the surprising majority of 350 to 15, the appearance of a new best-seller, Kate Millett's *Sexual Politics,* and numerous other books and articles in major magazines have brought the new revolution to public attention. Many who are aware of it are apt to smile at it as a passing fad, or as the fantastic behavior of a few queer people. Yet it is not likely soon to pass, though it will change its forms as is the usual way with revolutions.

But what, more precisely, is that new but old phenomenon commonly called the Women's Liberation Movement?

The movement takes many forms. One of its many organizations has the arresting title of WITCH (Women's International Terrorist Conspiracy from Hell). Others adopt such forms of protest against the usual ideas of femininity as the abolition of the bra, the taking of karate lessons, the boycott of Miss America contests, and protest *en masse* against women's magazines for catering to the more superficial and male-ensnaring aspects of feminine nature.[10] It is these protests which until recently have received the greatest publicity because of their startling nature, and they have doubtless hurt the movement by eliciting smiles or frowns.

A more temperate approach is that of NOW (National Organization of Women) which owes its origin chiefly to Mrs. Betty Friedan, whose book *The Feminine Mystique* appeared in 1963 and launched the neo-feminist movement of our time. The major concern of NOW is for equality of employment, pay, and promotion in the labor market.[11] That such equality, supposedly assured by Title VII of the Civil Rights Act of 1964, has been utterly lacking in practice is gradually permeating the mind of the American public.

Still another type of approach is that of the National Woman's Party. The main concern of this group is political action, and it is related to the preceding in that its lobby worked valiantly for the inclusion of the word "sex" in Title VII of the Civil Rights Act of 1964. It has stanchly opposed efforts to revise the Act by omitting "sex" on the pleas that this invalidates "protective" legislation. Which is more important, say these women, to be kept from having to lift weights of a specified amount and to work overtime (both of which women are often able and willing to do), or to continue to be underpaid, denied merited promotions and executive positions, and then be the first to be laid off when unemployment strikes?

The main concern of the National Woman's Party, both of late and for many years, has been to secure an Equal Rights Amendment to the United States Constitution, which would prohibit sex discrimination in all areas and not solely in employment as Title VII would do if it were enforced. It was a great victory for the National Woman's Party when this Amendment, bottled up in the Judiciary Committee for 47 years, passed the House of Representatives by such a resounding majority on August 10, 1970. It struck snags in the Senate and was temporarily withdrawn. Though its ultimate fate is not known at the time of this writing, its sponsorship in the 91st Senate by more than eighty members gives evidence that it has passed far beyond being the dream of a few concerned women.

3. Women in the churches

By a curious paradox, the church has long declared the equality of all persons before God, and its gospel has been one of the primary democratizing agencies of the Western world. In the Orient as well, its missionary movement has stirred and reinforced the demand for freedom, equality, and justice. Yet in the church itself, conservatism has prevailed in regard to the place of women in its leadership. This is especially true in regard to its ordained ministry and its major policy-making agencies.

What has caused this resistance? In part, it has been due to biblical literalism and the force of certain prohibitions stemming from, or at least attributed to, Paul. Those who do not wish to see women ordained to the Christian ministry can cite all sorts of subtle theological reasons why it should not be done, which we shall examine later. Some find practical barriers, of greater or less importance. Probably, however, in our time the principal factor is the pull of a long tradition. The fact that women have never occupied major places in the intellectual and administrative ranks of the church has made it extremely difficult to break through the barriers erected over many centuries.

As a result, the church has lagged behind all the other principal social institutions in its admission of qualified women to leadership on terms of equality with men. Some thirty years ago I was asked to speak on the place of women in the church at a nationwide Methodist gathering—the only woman on a roster of thirty-six speakers on the program of the Assembly. I was asked, as I presume others were, to submit an advance copy of my address for publicity purposes—not, I am sure, for censorship. A wise friend who read my manuscript in advance of its delivery caught the sentence, "The church is the last stronghold of male dominance." "That," she said, "is certainly true. But it will do no good to say it. It will only offend the men, who will not then listen to the rest of the address." I took her advice and omitted this sentence from my speech. But the copy of the address had already been sent to the publicity office! This proved to be the punch line which apparently got into every newspaper which reported the Assembly. For the next three weeks I received clippings from friends all the way from Maine to California bearing such headlines as "Dr. Harkness scores the church; calls it the last stronghold of male dominance."

How is it now? The truth of the statement continues, though there has been softening all along the line. Officially, many more of the American Protestant denominations are willing to ordain women than was true thirty years ago, though conservatism in congregations still makes the number of women who are ministers in local parishes a tiny minority. Most of the seminaries have opened their doors to women, though it is often expected that "woman's place" in the world of religion is either in Christian education, as a minister's wife and hence unpaid coworker, or in the voluntary activities of the local women's society. In most major Protestant bodies, women may now be delegates to their denomination's national assembly, but the number is always a small minority. Despite the fact that well over half of the churches' lay membership consists of women, and the further fact that the women's organizations are almost invariably stronger and more active than the corresponding men's organizations if these exist, lay representation in governing bodies is overwhelmingly that of lay men.

Within the past thirty years, women have been finding opportunities formerly closed to them opening in many fields, including the church. Yet is it not still true that "the church is the last stronghold of male dominance"?

I do not wish to give the impression that none of the male leaders of the church see in it a place of equality for the talents of women. A considerable number, both among Protestants and among some Catholic dissidents from traditional authority, recognize that the church has not exemplified the equalitarian implications of its gospel. Were not this the case, we should not now have some eighty Protestant denominations, large and small, that officially ordain women.[12] Except for a few instances like the Quakers, Salvation Army, and the Disciples of Christ which have never had official sex barriers to women in their ministry, this would not have come about unless men had voted to remove the barriers. Nevertheless, it appears that most men in the churches, all the way from the rank-and-file lay men to the bishops, think women have all the opportunities they need and cannot see what the fuss is all about.

This was brought vividly to my attention recently when an outstanding bishop of my church was addressing a large group of women of whom I was one. After speaking of various Christian causes of our time to which we might well give our concern and service, he exclaimed, "There's the Women's Liberation Front! I don't know what you women want; you have everything now! But if you can show me what you want, I'll try to help you get it." Nobody interrupted the speaker to tell him "what women want," though plenty of those present could have told him. I cite this incident because it illustrates the present situation. Vast numbers of male churchmen, along with others outside of churches, appear to think that women have everything they need, and many are not so willing as the bishop to try to help them get it.

An indication of this is the disproportionate scarcity of women in such organs of the church as have a place for lay representation. To illustrate again, the very influential Program Council of my church is made up of fifteen bishops, twenty ministers, and thirty-five laymen —seven of the latter from each of its five Jurisdictions. The enabling legislation specifies that, of the seven laymen, "at least two shall be women." Result? Ten women out of the seventy, with the minimum number having been elected in every Jurisdiction. When two women members of the General Conference attempted to secure a somewhat more even balance among the lay representatives, their efforts were greeted with laughter.

As I listened to this foiled attempt, I was vividly reminded of an earlier occasion. In the General Conference of 1952, after repeated attempts to secure full clergy rights for women in successive General Conferences had been rejected, the matter came up in its closing moments. It was passed over rapidly with the usual rejection, to the accompaniment of considerable laughter. I may be divulging some unwritten history when I say that some of the women present resolved that it was no longer to be treated as a laughing matter! The consequence was action by the Woman's Division of Christian Service which resulted in over 2,000 petitions on the subject to the General Conference of 1956; between three and four hours of vigorous debate on the floor of the Conference, mainly between men on both sides of the issue; and a vote for the full eradication of official sex discrimination in the ministry of The Methodist Church. (I purposely sat in silence, for there were able and discerning men to carry the issue, and I had long before learned that this is often the surest way to get something passed.)

With these incidents stored in my memory, I was interested to discover that the men of my denomination are not the only ones who sometimes treat it as a joke when women try to present their case in an ecclesiastical arena. In a news report of the United Presbyterian U.S.A. General Assembly of 1970, this passage appeared:

In the case of presentations from women (from the Women's Liberation Union and the assembly's own standing committee on women) even benign neglect or polite in-attentiveness were too much for many of the male commissioners. Both presentations were met with laughter and clever commentary from men who evidently considered the discussion of women's rights a comic diversion from their serious business.[18]

I do not believe that Methodist or Presbyterian men are more lacking in chivalry than others. But what, after all, is chivalry? When women are asking for something which the men do not think they need or ought to have, perhaps it seems to them more chivalrous to make a joke of the matter than to tell the women, point-blank, to shut up and mind their own business. But sometimes a joke backfires.

4. *How shall we proceed?*

Having been somewhat personal in the immediately preceding pages, perhaps I should continue in this vein and indicate the stance from which this book will be presented. I have never considered myself a "suffragette" or a "feminist" in the usual connotation of these terms, though I believe that "feminist" which has become a dirty word should be redeemed. I have never taken part in a demonstration, not even those of "Women Strike for Peace" or the "Jeannette Rankin Brigade" demanding an end to the war in Vietnam, a cause which calls forth my deep sympathy. This may be due to cowardice on my part or to a deep-seated conformism. Or it may be because I have suffered relatively little from sex discrimination. I felt it earlier in my professional life in the fact that the colleges had comparatively few places open to women teachers, and that even the women's colleges usually preferred men. Since I began teaching theology at Garrett in 1940, and later at the Pacific School of Religion, my colleagues have never shown any indication of excluding me because of my sex, and they are among my warmest friends. If my students objected to being taught by a woman, they did not tell me of it. (One did, but he has since become a firm and long-time friend.) My church has given me far more opportunities and more recognition than I merit, and to write a "sour grapes" type of book is the last thing I want to do.

At the same time, there are plain facts that need to be stated, and some things that need to be done about them. I have long known this, and upon occasion have raised my voice for greater equality for women, particularly in the matter of the ministry. Naturally I was both surprised and gratified when in 1956, only a few weeks apart, both the Methodist General Conference and the Presbyterian General Assembly removed all official barriers in this field. I may have had a small part in this, but much less than I am sometimes given credit for. It was mainly due to two things: (1) the fine record of those able and courageous women who were already serving effectively in little parishes across the land as "accepted supply" pastors, and (2) the wisdom of the men who were willing to support full clergy status for women, because they saw that this was right.

At the fiftieth anniversary assembly of the American Association of Women Ministers in 1969 I gave two addresses. One of them, with a backward look at the nineteenth century, was entitled "Pioneer Women in the Ministry" and appeared in the Summer, 1970 issue of *Religion in Life*.[14] The other, looking toward the future, dealt with our hopes and how best to achieve them. This was unwritten and unpublished, but its six main points were summarized in *The Woman's Pulpit*.[15] To indicate the stance from which I am presenting this book, perhaps I cannot do better than to restate them.

1. We must maintain our feminity, never forgetting that we are women.
2. Be cooperative in spirit, working with men on all suitable occasions.
3. Trust our men friends (there are times when they can better speak for us than we can for ourselves).
4. Keep up with the times. Do not forget the lessons of history, but look to the future.
5. We must choose our priorities. The gospel is more important than women's rights.
6. Be faithful to your calling.

To sum up where we now stand, some affirmations may be made which will require further elaboration in the pages which follow.

Most women today look upon their homes as their first responsibility, but not as their sole sphere of useful or satisfying activity. Many who work outside their homes want creative occupations to utilize their skills on terms of full equality with men.

Women may or may not appreciate the right to vote, and few know or think much about the long struggle which secured it for them. The idea of a woman as President is still a remote possibility, but many women believe that their sex is entitled to a larger place in politics and government than has been accorded.

In the churches many women find spheres of useful service in the voluntary women's organizations. The churches as a whole would be very much poorer in both means and vitality without them. But these same women would like to see their sex represented more fully in the various echelons of church government. With more women than men in church membership, they should occupy more than the present minor place in church leadership.

Wonen in the ministry? We have noted that this has advanced to the point where women may prepare for it in the Protestant seminaries, and in a considerable number of denominations they may be ordained. This is not yet true in the Roman Catholic and Orthodox churches, though there are stirrings in this direction. But women as parish ministers? Only a few have found an initial welcome. Those receiving such appointments are usually respected and beloved upon acquaintance. Meanwhile, churches languish for lack of an adequate supply of dedicated and well-trained men to man them.

Women as teachers of theology or other branches of religion? Or as writers in this field? Here the Roman Catholic women have the edge on the rest of us, having found a virtue in necessity. Not being admitted to seminaries designed as preparation for the priesthood, they created schools of their own, which in turn have provided teaching opportunities for the best qualified of their graduates. As a result some of the best writing now being done in the field of our inquiry is by Catholic women, though there are excellent books by Protestant women also to which the reader is referred.[16] Meanwhile, the other teaching positions formerly open in small numbers to women have become virtually negligible in the present oversupply of male candidates.

If the bishop previously referred to should chance to read this book, I hope he may discover that the women of today do not "have everything," and that there are legitimate yearnings, consistent with the Christian gospel, which he can help them to secure. To this enterprise let us now move forward.

II A long heritage

Never since the beginning of history have women been regarded as having full equality with men. Whether it can be affirmed that women have always been in subjection to men, or have always had an inferior status, depends on the meaning attached to these somewhat ambiguous terms. Since the age of feudal knighthood women in the Western world have been viewed as entitled to a measure of chivalry, and more recently as having considerable importance in the family and in private life. Throughout the centuries there have occasionally been great queens, great female saints, and now and then a famous female figure in other walks of life. But this does not alter the fact that for the rank and file of women—the great masses of the female half of humanity—subordination and a denial of opportunities enjoyed by men have been the established order of existence. A survey of the centuries corroborates the judgment of the late British woman preacher, A. Maude Royden, "When all exceptions are allowed their full weight, and all the influences of affection, convention, decency, and humanity taken into account, the outstanding fact in the history of women has been their universal subordination to men." [1]

1. *The early centuries*

A look at the status of women in primitive society and the earlier periods of civilization may at first glance seem irrelevant because those years were far away and long ago. The mood of the present is to concentrate on the present, whether one belongs to "the Now generation" or a somewhat older age group. Yet what happened in the past—even the long past—is by no means irrelevant to our understanding of the present. This is true in many fields, but in reference to the problem of the status of women it is especially relevant for two reasons: (1) the subordination of women today is a direct inheritance from subordination in the past in every field—domestic, economic, political, or religious, and (2) the social mores of the Bible have been a powerful force in shaping the sexual mores of the Western world. Not only does the Bible bring a fresh spiritual insight on what should be the conditions of human living, but its social setting is placed very largely in the accepted patterns of life in primitive and early Middle East society. Thus in spite of a greatly changed world in other respects, these patterns to no small degree have projected an influence into the modern world in regard to the position of women.

For these reasons we shall begin this study with a review of these ancient social mores. They are presented at greater length and placed in a wider setting in my earlier book, *The Sources of Western Morality*.[2] Yet even a few brief notations may help to clarify the picture.

Occasionally one finds feminists who, apparently longing for a return to some Golden Age of the past, cite the existence of a matriarchate in primitive society. Yet the term is misleading, for there never was a time when social custom generally sanctioned the *rule* of women. According to the best anthropological evidence available, there apparently was a time in some primitive

37

cultures when inheritance was transmitted through the mother's side of the house. Women were then under the authority of fathers, brothers, and uncles rather than husbands, for the woman remained among her own kin while the often absent husband had to care for his own sisters and their children. This awkward arrangement, more accurately called the maternal family or mother-right rather than a matriarchate, did not guarantee any unusual powers to the woman. L. P. Hobhouse says in *Morals in Evolution,* an old book but still a classic in its field, "Along with mother-right, and where it most flourishes, it is perfectly possible for the position of women to be as low as the greatest misogynist could desire." [3]

This type of family did not last long. It passed over into the far more typical family in which wives and children were regarded as the property of the husband and father, and were very much under his rule. This survived to lay foundations which have permeated the civilized world, and its traces are to be found today in advanced as well as in less developed societies.

In the patriarchal family, which is clearly the background against which the Old Testament was written, the bride was selected by family arrangement, often with no previous acquaintance between bride and groom. She was then secured (one may as well say bought) by gifts of cattle, jewelry, or other goods, and in later periods by money. There is a typical account of an arranged marriage and bride-price in the story of Isaac's courtship of Rebekah where we read, "Then the servant took ten of his master's camels and departed, taking all sorts of choice gifts from his master; and he arose, and went to Mesopotamia, to the city of Nahor" (Gen. 24:10). The story as a whole is not quite typical, for the strong-minded Rebekah seems to have taken more initiative in the subsequent arrangements than most brides. Sometimes a poor man could win his bride by services; this is illustrated by Jacob's long service to Laban for the wooing of Rachel (Gen. 29). In either case, the bride entered her husband's family and became his possession. Such arranged marriages were not unlike those still found in advanced forms of oriental society.

Within these early mores both polygamy and concubinage were common practices, as we shall have occasion to note later in surveying the position of the women of Israel. Not only concubines but wives were sometimes acquired by capture as the outcome of tribal warfare. This is illustrated in the biblical story of the seizure of the daughters of Shiloh to provide wives for the Benjaminites (Judg. 21:16-24).

There were variations to some degree within the patriarchal family, but one factor remained constant. The wife was the husband's property. She must fulfill his sexual desires, bear him children, preferably sons, tend his household, and obey his wishes. As occasion required, she must use her sexual charms to advance his prestige or to trick his enemies. As agriculture developed, she was often expected to work in the fields as well as to "keep the home fires burning." There is some evidence that agriculture originated when women first planted some wild seeds in the patch of ground around the fires where they cooked the meat brought home by their husbands from the hunt or from the grazing flocks.[4]

While mutual love was seldom, if ever, the initial basis of a patriarchal family, it doubtless sometimes developed, as in the royal marriages of many centuries or the arranged marriages of today in much of the Third World. Yet whether or not love was present, the wife must honor and obey her husband. Submissive service and faithful compliance with his wishes were, and are, the primary marks of the patriarchal family.

In the preceding paragraphs, the past tense has been used. But with some relatively minor changes, is not much of the same structure found in the contemporary European or American household? Brides are no longer overtly bought or captured; the contracting parties usually have considerable autonomy in the union. Yet the union, once consummated, is often marked either by a male assumption of patriarchal control or by a female defiance of it which is a recent development in a long history. As a result the marriage breaks up, usually with fault on both sides. In earlier days women submitted and suffered, whether silently or not; in the present a new sense of a woman's right to full personhood comes into the picture. Hence, the Women's Liberation Movement.

To look now at the great civilizations of the ancient world, we find that in the earliest of these, the Egyptian, individual women attained to some prominence. The status of women was higher there than in most early societies. There is the story of a great early monotheist, the Pharaoh Amenhotep IV, who changed his name to Ikhnaton (or Akhnaton) to renounce allegiance to Ammon. Ikhnaton loved his beautiful wife and showed her great honor. How much of his deeply religious and poetic spirit he owed to her we can only conjecture. It is certain that Egypt produced one great queen, Hatshepsut, who was the first great woman ruler of history. Yet what are we to make of the fact that she is represented on her monuments in masculine garb with a long beard? Her successor Thothmes III apparently did not like the idea of a woman ruler, for he smashed many of her monuments and placed a sheath of masonry around her obelisk to conceal the inscriptions of her exploits. However, gravitation foiled his attempt to keep them concealed forever, for in time the masonry fell away and the inscriptions have revealed her greatness to modern archaeologists.

If sacred legend is to be trusted, both the unnamed wife of Potiphar who tried to seduce Joseph and got him imprisoned when he resisted (Gen. 39) and the likewise unnamed daughter of the Pharaoh who became the foster mother of Moses (Exod. 2:1-10) were picturesque feminine figures. Asenath, whom Joseph married by the Pharaoh's arranging, was an Egyptian girl, the daughter of a priest in a rich and influential priesthood, and therefore doubtless of considerable prestige (Gen. 41: 45). There are no archaeological remains to tell us more about them. This may not matter greatly, for the ordinary life of the ordinary Egyptian woman was apparently rather humdrum and not very different from the lot of women in other patriarchal families.

When we turn to the next great civilization, the Babylonian, we have a priceless treasure in the Code of Hammurabi, which tells among many other matters of justice how women ought to be treated. This is not to say that they were thus treated, for such codes are usually in advance of the prevailing situation, indicating wrongs that require correction. Yet the Code shows a surprising concern for "women's rights."

Monogamous marriage is presupposed, though if a wife does not bear him children her husband may take a concubine. Marriage was by contract, and a woman could divorce her husband, though not so easily as he could divorce her. Furthermore, she could divorce him not only for infidelity, but for cruelty or neglect if she could prove that she had been a good wife. Though a man could divorce his wife at will, he must return her dowry and provide for the support of her children. As elsewhere marriages were arranged for a bride price, but a woman could retain her dowry and pass it on to her children. Not even a concubine who had borne children could be put away without support for herself and her children. When one considers the long battle in the Western world for women to have legal control of their property and to secure their freedom from a soul-stifling marriage, the Code of Hammurabi is definitely in advance of its time.

2. *The women of Israel*

Israel was the next great nation to emerge on the world scene. In this chapter we shall deal only with the social attitudes and standards of morality in the Old Testament. The theological deductions which may be drawn from the stories of the Creation and the Fall, and from the worship of a single male deity with no goddesses or priestesses as in the surrounding religions of the time, must be reserved for a later discussion.

Even with this limitation, the consideration of attitudes toward women among the Hebrews is complex because of changes in the course of the nation's varied history, with occasional examples of outstanding women and fine family relations amid a prevailing sordidness. The loose sexuality and tight male dominance reflected in many historical narratives are at variance with what the later codes suggest of extreme penalties for both sexes in sexual infractions. And as if this were not complication enough, much of the writing was done several centuries after the events are said to have occurred, and in the process of compiling and editing old tales the text must have taken on some of the writers' and editors' opinions. To judge Israel's moral history in regard to women as either good or bad without qualification is bound to court distortion. Yet in spite of these difficulties, some presentation and assessment of main trends must be attempted.

The Old Testament affords many examples of life in a patriarchal society. The patriarchal period begins with Abraham and extends to Moses with his deliverance of his people from bondage in Egypt and his welding of a nomadic tribe into a nation with a sense of common identity and destiny. Yet the marks of a patriarchal society with its arranged marriages, subordination of women except as the bearers of sons, and almost total male dominance, lasted much longer.

This remained the prevailing pattern of family life even to the end of the Old Testament period. Yet within it there are conspicuous variations from the norm. Elsie Culver in *Women in the World of Religion*[5] suggests that in the patriarchal period the position of women was higher than it became later. I doubt this to have been the case, though it is certain that in tales of this era some outstanding female personalities appear. Although Abraham was a polygamist, as was Jacob also, Sarah was a person in her own right and the slave concubine Hagar elicits our sympathy. Rebekah not only helped along her wedding arrangements when the servant came to take her to Isaac, but it was she who took the upper hand in scheming for her favorite son Jacob to get the birthright away from his twin brother Esau. Jacob's long service to win Rachel—a second seven years after he had been obliged to take Leah at the end of the first seven—is both a dramatic and a tender love story. But in spite of these fascinating stories, the ordinary life style of the women of this era as of later periods was probably one of subjection to their fathers and husbands, with some control by their brothers added.

Several Old Testament women are designated as prophetesses, and we must take account of these as of special importance. They were not priestesses, and there is no indication of their participating in the rituals of worship. They were interpreters of the word of the Lord, which meant in actuality that they were important female leaders.

With the emergence of Moses comes the story of his sister Miriam, whose cleverness as a child was responsible for the royal rearing of Moses in the Pharaoh's court (Exod. 2:1-10). As an adult she was considered a prophetess, though she lost favor by joining Aaron against Moses and was threatened with leprosy (Num. 12). The Song of Miriam (Exod. 15:20-21) which celebrates the successful crossing of the Red Sea is perhaps the oldest bit of poetry in the Bible.

Exceeding Miriam in both poetic and political power was Deborah in the period of the judges. Also referred to as a prophetess, she was in reality a great political and military leader, who with the help of her male assistant Barak defeated Sisera, a Canaanite leader, and thus won a decisive victory for her people. The Song of Deborah (Judg. 5) celebrates this victory, and in it tells the somewhat gruesome story of how another strong-minded woman, Jael, enticed Sisera into her tent to rest and then drove a tent peg through his temple as he lay asleep. Deborah had a husband, but who remembers his name? We are told in Judg. 4:4, "Now Deborah, a prophetess, the wife of Lappidoth, was judging Israel at that time." Since Lappidoth is never mentioned again, one may guess who ruled that household!

Another prophetess, Huldah, at a later date was apparently a very important woman, though we are told less about her than about Deborah. In the reign of King Josiah in 621 B.C. it was decided to repair the dilapidated parts of the Jerusalem temple. In the process a "book of the law" was found, which became the basis of extensive reforms and was destined to become the greater part of the book of Deuteronomy. Upon its discovery the king was greatly impressed with it. Not being quite sure of its divine authority, he sent to "inquire of the Lord for me, and for the people, and for all Judah, concerning the words of this book that has been found" (II Kings 22:13). Straightway it was taken to Huldah the prophetess for a decision! She not only endorsed its divine authenticity but gave some stern warnings if its injunctions were not carried out, whereupon the king launched the reforms (II Kings 22:14-20).

We wish we knew more about Huldah. She was a contemporary of Jeremiah, though apparently somewhat older. Why did the decision in this important matter rest with her when there were plenty of men who could have been consulted? The only plausible answer is that she seems to have been considered an expert in discerning the words of the Lord, for the king accepted her judgment. If we prize the arts of peace above those of war, Huldah may have been a greater woman than Deborah.

About a fourth prophetess, Noadiah, we know even less. Explicit statement about her is limited to one verse in the account of the rebuilding of the wall of Jerusalem by Nehemiah after the return of the exiles from Jerusalem. Here we find Nehemiah saying, "Remember

Tobiah and Sanballat, O my God, according to these things that they did, and also the prophetess Noadiah and the rest of the prophets who wanted to make me afraid" (Neh. 6:14).

A woman important enough to frighten Nehemiah? Or at least to make him mention her as an opponent? There must be a story behind that!

By piecing together portions of Ezekiel, Ezra, and Nehemiah, Mrs. Culver in *Women in the World of Religion*[6] has presented an explanation which is at least historically plausible. It was mainly the people of prestige and wealth who had been carried away into Babylon. The poor and less important people who were left behind adjusted to the situation and found they could get along well enough without the others. When the exiles returned, they took over the situation in the name of the Lord and started to build a wall around Jerusalem. Opposition developed among those who preferred peace with their neighbors to Jewish exclusiveness. In Ezekiel 13 we learn of false prophets "saying 'Peace,' when there is no peace; and . . . when the people build a wall, these prophets daub it with whitewash" (Ezek. 13:10). Dire prophecies of rain, wind, hailstones, and finally destruction are promised them. Among these disturbers are a group of women who wear wristbands and veils for identification, and they are charged with "hunting down souls" and with having "disheartened the righteous" (Ezek. 13:17-23). Translated into modern terms, this seems to mean that they had been recruiting for a confrontation against the Establishment. If Noadiah was their leader, no wonder Nehemiah thought her worth mentioning!

There are other dramatic stories about women in the Old Testament. There is the familiar story of Ruth and her fidelity to her mother-in-law Naomi, which culminated in her marriage to Boaz, a distant relative of her first husband. They are named in Matthew 1:5 as ancestors of Jesus. There is Queen Esther's courageous intercession for her people before her husband, the Persian King Ahasuerus. There are the adventures of David's various wives, of whom Abigail (I Sam. 25:14-42), Michal (I Sam. 18:20-27; 19:11-17; II Sam. 6:20-23), and Bathsheba (II Sam. 11:2-5; 12:15-24) are the most famous. We cannot linger with them but must return to the main stream of sexual morals and practices.

This main stream contains numerous pictures not usually preached about in churches or presented in the Sunday schools. The author of a definitive classic on the moral life of the Hebrews, J. M. Powis Smith, says this of the early historical narratives:

"Polygamy was the order of the day. Samuel's mother was one of two wives (I Sam. 1:2); Gideon's father had 'many wives' (Judg. 8:30); David had eight wives who are individually mentioned (I Sam. 18:20, 27; 25:39,43; II Sam. 3:2-5, 13; 11:27; I Kings 1:1-4), and he married yet more wives in Jersualem (II Sam. 5:13-16, and when he left Jerusalem in haste, fleeing from Absalom, he left ten concubines behind him in the city (II Sam. 15:16). Solomon's uxorious proclivities are notorious. Of course, Solomon must be given credit for political and commercial aims to the accomplishment of which the marriages with foreign princesses were a necessary means. Inherent in the system of polygamy are certain evils which are exemplified in the family life of this period. There was rivalry and enmity between the wives of Elkanah (I Sam. 1:5-8). The family tie among the children of different wives was very weak. Gideon's son Abimelech slew all but one of his half-brothers, seventy in number, and set himself up as king of Shechem (Judg. 9:5, 6) . . . . Faithfulness to the marriage bond did not weigh heavily upon husbands, and a general looseness of sexual relations prevailed. Samson . . . visited a harlot of Gaza (Judg. 16:1) and appears to have suffered no blame; Jephthah's mother was a woman of similar record (Judg. 11:1) . . . . David's sin with Bathsheba is condemned indeed, but the ground of the condemnation is the wrong done to her husband, and not any wrong to Bathsheba or himself (II Sam. chap. 11) . Under the circumstances, women as such seem to have had little consideration. Chivalry was an unknown quantity. . . ." [7]

There are more pages of such illustrations. But we must leave them to look at the law codes, which reveal both sex discrimination and an attempt to secure some measure of sexual purity and justice.

The most familiar of all of these is, of course, the Decalogue, or Ten Commandments. Whether or not the story of their having been given to Moses graven on tablets of stone is literal history, they are of great importance both for what they contain and for the authority they have had through the centuries. They appear twice, the earliest form being found in Exodus 20:2-17 and a later version in Deuteronomy 5:6-21 as part of the Deuteronomic "book of the law."

In both forms the fifth commandment is the injunction, "Honor your father and your mother." The mention of the mother is important as indicating something of her importance. But why are parents to be honored? Apparently from self-interest—that one may have long life, and the version in Deuteronomy is even more explicit, for it adds "that it may go well with you." This hardly suggests a loving and selfless concern for either parent!

The remaining commandments fix attention on very vital needs of any culture—the preservation of human life, family integrity, property rights, truth-telling, the curbing of covetous desires. So essential are they that we may well regard them as God-given even if they came through Moses or, as many biblical scholars believe, emerged out of the growing social consciousness of the people.

Two of these relate particularly to the family situation. The seventh commandment, "You shall not commit adultery," is of universal and timeless importance. As we shall note presently, the later codes made rigid requirements for its observance. But what of the tenth where "you shall not covet your neighbor's wife" places the wife in exactly the same category as the neighbor's house, his servants, and his cattle? The two versions differ slightly in that the later one places the wife first in the list; let us hope that by that time she had come to seem more important than the house. Yet either form implies that one's wife is one's property as indeed she was assumed to be.

The Old Testament contains three much longer and more detailed law codes: the Covenant Code (Exod. 20:23-23:33), which immediately follows the Exodus Decalogue and dates from the ninth or eighth century B.C.; the Deuteronomic Code (Deut. 12-26) of the late seventh century; and the Holiness Code (Lev. 17-26) of a more ritualistic and stringent nature compiled after the return from exile. In all these there are provisions for the protection of a woman's chastity and for other aspects of sexual morality.

In the Covenant Code, if a virgin were seduced, the seducer must provide a dowry and marry her, or if the girl's father refused the marriage, he must make a money payment in any case (Exod. 22:16-17). The obvious reason is that the girl's monetary value as a potential bride has been thus impaired. Likewise, if a pregnant woman is accidentally injured and a miscarriage results, the person who caused the injury must pay a fine to the husband (Exod. 21:22). (The lost infant might have been a son!) But if more serious harm results, the *lex talionis* prevails. A man may sell his daughter as a slave, but not to a foreign people (Exod. 21:7-8). Plural wives are permitted, but they must be properly cared for (Exod. 21:10-11).

In the Deuteronomic Code women fare somewhat better. Women slaves as well as men are to be released every seventh year and go out liberally provided for (Deut. 15:12-17). A man may divorce his wife, but only through a written bill of divorce, and she may remarry (Deut. 24:1-2). For rape of a betrothed maiden the man pays with his life; if she is unbetrothed, he pays her father fifty shekels and must marry her (Deut. 22:23-29). Adultery now becomes a capital offense for both parties (Deut. 22:22). The reason given suggests both its frequency and its stain on the national honor, "so you shall purge the evil from Israel."

In the Holiness Code, severe penalties for sexual offenses are spelled out at greater length. Adultery remains a capital offense, though with a female slave it requires only a guilt offering for its expiation (Lev. 19:20-22). Incest, homosexuality, and intercourse with a beast must also receive the death penalty (Lev. 20:11-16). For various other types of sexual irregularity, the penalty is to be "cut off from among their people," or to be childless (Lev. 20:17-21).

How rigidly were these penalties enforced? The historical sections do not tell us. It is significant that the only account we have of a stoning for adultery is found in the New Testament, where the offender-victim is a woman (John 8:3-11). It is doubtful that many male culprits were actually put to death for such sexual offenses. Yet there is an austerity about these codes which left its effects. Through the centuries more than a few persons, particularly if they were women, have been "cut off from among their people" because of such aberrations from the norm.

There were both lights and shadows in Israel's sex standards, and some changes as the years progressed. Polygamy was practically gone by New Testament times, to reappear later in Mohammedanism. But one thing never changed—the superior power and authority of the male. Though it lies beyond the Old Testament period, there is congruity between the thought of this era and the morning prayer which came to be used in orthodox Jewish synagogues, blessing God "who hath not made me a Gentile . . . a slave . . . or a woman." [8]

I have reserved to the end of this section an early story of domestic relations which is of special importance because it has cast its shadow into political and national relations on the contemporary scene.

This is the story of Abraham, his two wives,[9] and his two sons Ishmael and Isaac. With some repetition from a combining of sources, it is told in Genesis 16; 17:15-21; 18:9-15; and 21:1-21, and in spite of other matter being interspersed it is still a very dramatic story. Abraham, finding his wife Sarah to be barren and fearing he might die without an heir, with Sarah's consent took her maid Hagar as his wife. She bore him Ishmael, to Abraham's great joy and Hagar's pride. Then the tide turned, and Sarah "dealt harshly" with Hagar. Although both Abraham and Sarah were old, she then by divine intervention

was able to conceive in spite of her years and to bear
Isaac. Meanwhile the Covenant, so vital to Hebrew history, had been established between God and Abraham.

The jealousy of Sarah for her own son Isaac and the
fear that Ishmael might also become Abraham's heir in
spite of the divine promise caused her, with Abraham's
reluctant permission, to send Hagar and her son out into
the desert, the wilderness of Beersheba.[10] The food and
water provided by Abraham gave out, and they would
have perished had not Yahweh miraculously preserved
them by showing them a well. Furthermore, the angel of
the Lord promised that Ishmael would become the father of a multitude of descendants and a great nation
(Gen. 16:10; 21:17-18).

Is this only a tale from the long past? Legend tells
that Ishmael became the father of the Arabs as Isaac
of the Jews. To the present there are both a mosque
and a synagogue over the reputed burial place of Abraham in Hebron, while two groups engaged in a bitter
contest that imperils the modern world can both trace
their ancestry to Abraham and claim to be his legitimate
heir.

3. Women of Greece and Rome

Turning from the most religious of the ancient civilizations to the most brilliant, we find in Greece that, although male dominance prevails, the situation is in
some respects quite different. We must resist the tendency to generalize, for different types and classes of
women appear. At least two of these have left marks
extending out of the long past to the present.

The ordinary virtuous, faithful, married woman left
no such mark. She was for the most part secluded and

untaught. She was completely under the authority of her husband and seldom could exercise even the meager rights the law allowed her. Greece had some beautiful women, but the most that can be said of their contribution to history is that the ten years' Trojan War was fought because one of them was the wife of Menelaus, the king of Sparta.

A second class of Greek women were the hetaerae. These were high-class prostitutes, courtesans who often supplied professional entertainment as well as sexual satisfaction to Greek men who could afford their services. Such liaisons varied as to permanence, but the fact that the same stem is found in the word hetaerism which refers to concubinage in primitive societies, suggests that the hetaera could advance from being a talented promiscuous prostitute to what might now be called a mistress.

How do they effect our present society? By a biblical channel. The hetaerae went out in public unveiled; they did not hesitate to speak in public, without husbands to suppress them or do the talking for them. Paul was eager not to have the women of the early Christian churches confused with them. Furthermore, the hetaerae of Corinth were connected with the worship of Aphrodite, the pagan goddess of love. Hence, it is not at all surprising that we find Paul writing to the church at Corinth, "The women should keep silent in the churches. For they are not permitted to speak, but should be subordinate, as even the law says. If there is anything they desire to know, let them ask their husbands at home. For it is shameful for a woman to speak in church" (I Cor. 14:34-35). To this day, these words are quoted as barriers to women in the ministry!

Another way in which a group of Greek women have

cast their long shadow into the present is also of a sexual nature. Homosexuality was very prevalent in Greece, as is evident from numerous references to it in Plato's dialogues, and while most of these persons were males there were females also. Some of these were talented and brilliant persons, including a group from the island of Lesbos of whom the poetess Sappho was the most outstanding. Hence, the word lesbian in our present English vocabulary.

How did Greek men regard Greek women? Doubtless for the most part as men of every period have—as indispensable but inferior beings. However, from two of the greatest philosophers of all time we have diametrically opposite opinions. Plato in his ideal Republic would have complete sex equality, with women taking their places along with men not only in education but in service in battle and in the highest offices of the State. Aristotle, on the other hand, ranked women along with slaves as being by nature inferior beings, and regarded them as existing only for the bearing and rearing of children. In the major contests of the sexes today, either side may quote distinguished authority.

In Rome, the status of women is a mixed picture. On the one hand, the Roman matron apparently enjoyed a greater degree of freedom than in any other ancient civilization. She was less secluded, more free to occupy a recognized place in society. She was often the respected mistress of a great household with considerable authority in it. But this does not mean that she had anything like full sex equality.

Here as elsewhere, a distinction must be drawn between earlier and later stages. An important feature of early Roman society was the *patria potestas*. This was the absolute power of the father over his children, even to the power of life and death and extending into their adult life. The result was infanticide, which was still being practiced in the time of the Empire and has its political counterpart in Herod's massacre of the male babies at the time of the birth of Jesus (Matt. 2:16-17). What was the place of the mother in this? It must many times have gone counter to all her maternal feelings, but there is no evidence that she had the power to intervene.

Both the *patria potestas* and infanticide gradually faded out. But still the political rights of women ranged from slender to nonexistent. It was not until the rise of Stoicism that much change took place. As the humane spirit of Stoicism, with its doctrine of the natural equality of all persons, became a vital force, this affected the status of women. "Many of the disabilities placed upon woman by the earlier law were removed; children were emancipated in a measure from the now unreasonable authority of the father; and the slave was placed under the protection of the law and safeguarded against the worst brutalities of a cruel master." [11]

In both Greece and Rome, esteem for the female principle appears more clearly in divine than in human society. The pantheon of deities included great goddesses. Among them were Juno, the wife of Jupiter and mother of Mars (war), Vulcan (fire), and Hebe (youth); Minerva, the virgin goddess of wisdom who sprang fullgrown from the forehead of Jupiter; Diana, goddess of the hunt; Ceres, goddess of earth and agriculture; Venus, the goddess of love and beauty; and Vesta, goddess of the hearth and home before whose altar six virgin priestesses, the famous Vestal Virgins, must keep the sacred fires aglow.

This mythology recognized that female attributes are

intimately related to all these vital pursuits of human society. Yet it was easier to worship these attributes in goddesses than to put them into operation in human society by a recognition of the equality of the sexes. So it has remained in a less mythological and more recent culture.

A new day was about to dawn which would usher in a Christian society. How were women to fare then? This must be our concern in the next chapters.

III Women in Christendom

With the coming of Jesus upon the human scene, a new vision of God, of man, and of human possibilities and responsibilities emerged. Through nearly twenty centuries his advent has altered the currents of society in the Western world, sometimes imperceptibly but indelibly. Our aim in this chapter is to assess the degree to which this vision has altered the status of women, both in the churches and in the larger society.

Christendom is defined in my dictionary as "that part of the world in which Christianity is generally professed; the Christian world." Has Christendom dissolved? Some would say so, or suggest this in speaking of a "post-Christian era." Certainly, a religious pluralism which makes a large place for secularism as the dominant social outlook is prevalent in our time. This was not always so. In this chapter we shall look at women in Christendom up to the nineteenth century only, when very significant new forces emerged.

1. Jesus and women

It is impossible to quote from the Gospels any explicit statement of Jesus on the position of women. This is not surprising, for neither do we find him saying anything about slavery, or racial equality, or democracy as a form of government, all of which have been profoundly affected by his ministry and teachings. Has the position of women been comparably affected? That must be our inquiry.

Without having specific words on the subject, we can nevertheless glean what Jesus thought about women from incidents and references which become meaningful when we see them in context. These are found particularly in his friendships, his ministries, and certain revealing conversations.

Jesus seems never to have married.[1] We need not assume from this that he was a misogynist, or that there was anything abnormal about his personal life, or that he ranked celibacy as a higher state than matrimony. While his family ties are not spelled out for us, there is reason enough for a single state in the fact that as the eldest son he must care for his mother and younger brothers and sisters after the death of Joseph. Then when his brothers could take over this responsibility, he felt profoundly the call of God to a special ministry.

He then summoned twelve male companions to share an intimate friendship and to travel about with him. The fact that no women were among the Twelve is sometimes claimed, in my judgment without warrant, to be a valid argument against the ordination of women to the Christian ministry in our time.[2] There is reason enough in the conditions of travel in that day and the social conventions of that time. Even today, for a woman to live by day and night in such an intimate circle of men might prove mutually embarrassing.

Nevertheless, Jesus had warm friends among women. In Luke's account of the travels of Jesus and the Twelve we learn that some women *did* go along, apparently as helpers in a little company of their own. Those enumerated are "some women who had been healed of evil spirits and infirmities: Mary, called Magdalene, from whom seven demons had gone out, and Joanna, the wife of Chuza, Herod's steward, and Susanna, and many others, who provided for them out of their means" (Luke 8:2-3). Friendship enabled these women to put up with hard conditions in an early form of "Ladies' Aid." Jesus did not turn them away.

Our clearest pictures of the friendships of Jesus with women are with Mary and Martha at the Bethany home, and with Mary of Magdala. In John's Gospel we are told with no equivocation, "Now Jesus loved Martha and her sister and Lazarus" (11:5). At the time of Lazarus' death it was Martha, the practical-minded homemaker, who first went out to meet Jesus and chided him for not being there to prevent the death. But Martha also rises to greatness in her affirmation of faith in the resurrection and in Jesus as the Christ, the Son of God (John 11:24-27). In Luke's story of a visit to the home in Bethany, Mary comes off the better of the two for having preferred to listen to the teaching of Jesus— an indication that he was willing a woman should thus listen and learn in spiritual matters (Luke 10:38-42). The depth of his friendship with the two sisters and Lazarus is evident from the fact that in their home he found hospitality in his last fateful week, and doubtless reassurance for his coming ordeal. Matthew and Mark tell the story of the woman in Bethany who anointed his feet with costly ointment to the indignation of the disciples, but only in John do we learn that this was Mary (Matt. 26:6-13; Mark 14:3-9; John 12:1-8).

A similar story, often confused with this one, appears in Luke 7:36-50. Here the setting is different and the bearer of the alabaster flask is a forgiven sinner. Was this Mary Magdalene? We do not know, but whoever she was, Jesus did not turn her away. We know of Mary

Magdalene's devotion as one of the supporting company with Jesus and the Twelve, being present at the crucifixion, coming early to the tomb on the resurrection morning, being the first to see the Risen Christ and to announce his presence to the disciples.

In view of the fact that Jesus lived in an atmosphere saturated with the idea of the subordination of women, such incidents indicate a radical difference in Jesus' estimate. Still more clearly is this evident in two stories in the Fourth Gospel, and however authentic the record may be, they are true to his spirit. These are of the encounter with the woman of Samaria at the well (John 4:1-30) and the woman taken in adultery (John 7:53–8:11). In the former the conversation ranges from asking for a drink of water to the highest theological insights, and the reaction of the returning disciples is very revealing, "They marveled that he was talking with a woman" (John 4:27). That wasn't done! But Jesus did it. In the story of the woman being stoned for adultery, the record may be spurious but it rings true both to Jewish custom and Jesus' transcendence of it as he says, "Neither do I condemn you; go, and do not sin again" (John 8:11).

Jesus healed women as freely as men, which indicates that his compassion could not be halted by sex differences. Among such incidents are the healing of Peter's mother-in-law (Mark 1:29-31); the little daughter of Jairus and on the way to his house the woman with a hemorrhage of twelve years' duration (Mark 5:21-43); the woman bent over with an infirmity for eighteen years, when he shocked the ruler of the synagogue by healing on the sabbath (Luke 13:10-17); and the daughter of the Syrophoenician woman, thereby extending his ministry beyond the bounds of race and nation as well as of sex (Mark 7:24-30).

The one recorded teaching of Jesus on sex relations has to do with divorce. Seen against its Old Testament background, there is more in this than appears on the surface. A Jewish man could divorce his wife quite easily with a bill of divorce, if "she finds no favor in his eyes because he has found some indecency in her" (Deut. 24:1). But there was no corresponding provision for a woman to divorce her husband. Jesus puts divorce on a much more exacting basis, the sacredness of the marriage relation. In Matthew's account, the only acceptable ground is unchastity (Matt. 19:3-9). In Mark's version, the earlier and probably more authentic record, divorce is forbidden to either party without exceptions, and each is equally guilty of adultery upon remarriage (Mark 10:2-12). This is doubtless a situation-conditioned element in Jesus' teaching, not a rigid prescription for all time, but what may be discerned from it is his view of the complete equality of the sexes in the marriage relation.

Jesus talked freely with women; he healed women; he protected the marriage bonds of women; he held individual women in firm friendship and high honor. Much of this was in defiance of prevailing custom. These indications make it clear that for Jesus there was no "second sex." He also regarded women as precious to God and open to the message which he felt called to proclaim. Because many responded, women found a vital place among his followers in the early church. We must look now at their position.

2. Women in the early church

In the book of Acts and in the Letters, there is a curious paradox as to the place of women in the early

Christian community. On the one hand, women seem
to have been very active in the work and worship of
the churches, far more than would normally have been
possible in Jewish or Greek society. As we shall note
presently, they received from Paul warm commendation
for their helpfulness. But on the other hand, we have the
restrictive words of Paul as to their speaking in church,
attending worship with heads unveiled, or seeking to
learn something through a channel other than their husbands. This same spirit as to the subordination of wom-
en in the churches is echoed in Ephesians in words that
Paul may or may not have written, and still more re-
strictively in I Timothy which he did not write. The
first of these two sides of the paradox has been largely
overlooked, while the second has been very influential
through the centuries in keeping women in subordination to men both in the church and in society.

We must look carefully at both sides of the record and
see if there is a way to bring them together without
complete inconsistency. Let us begin with the more favorable aspect.

It is in the first chapter of Acts that we begin to find
evidences of the active place of women in the nascent
church. In the account of the gathering of the eleven in
the upper room after the ascension of the risen Christ
we find these words after the enumeration of the disciples, "All these with one accord devoted themselves
to prayer, together with the women and Mary the
mother of Jesus, and with his brothers" (Acts 1:14).
With the exception of Mary we are not told which
women were there, but they must have been faithful
female followers of Jesus. Then the story moves directly
into the election of a successor to Judas. We are not told
whether the women voted, but there is no indication of

their dismissal. Peter, to be sure, addressed the company as "Brethren," but this means no more than a similar form of address in many mixed church gatherings of today.

Women were undoubtedly present at Pentecost, at least among the three thousand souls who responded to Peter's moving sermon and were baptized upon that occasion. In his quotation from Joel, Peter had said, "Your sons and your daughters shall prophesy." As a quotation this seems to me less important than what stands at the conclusion of the account of this birthday of the church, "And day by day, attending the temple together and breaking bread in their homes, they partook of food with glad and generous hearts, praising God and having favor with all the people" (Acts 2:46-47). The women were certainly present in these homes; it seems unlikely that they prepared the food and then were relegated to seclusion. The same may be said of the women in the numerous "house churches" mentioned throughout the record.

A number of women of distinction, of whom we know too little but enough to be sure they were not nonentities, appear in Acts and the Letters. There was Priscilla, Prisca for short, the wife of Aquila. The couple were close friends and associates of Paul. He lived with them for eighteen months in Corinth, sharing the trade of tent-making as well as their home. When Paul decided to go further "and with him Priscilla and Aquila" (Acts 18:18), the three went to Ephesus where Paul left them to visit other churches. In his absence an Alexandrian Jew by the name of Apollos came to Ephesus and began preaching in the synagogue with more zeal than understanding, "but when Priscilla and Aquila heard him, they took him and expounded to him the way of

God more accurately" (Acts 18:26). Almost always Priscilla is mentioned before Aquila. We find this again in Romans 16:3 in a possible reference to the riots at Ephesus, "Greet Prisca and Aquila, my fellow workers in Christ Jesus, who risked their necks for my life, to whom not only I but also all the churches of the Gentiles give thanks." Unquestionably Priscilla was quite a person! It has been suggested that she acted as Paul's editorial secretary, and even that she is the author of the anonymous letter to the Hebrews. For lack of sufficient evidence I do not press these points, but clearly she was a person of much ability. Yet when I began to look her up in the commentaries, what I found was "Priscilla. See Aquila."

Then there was Lydia, the merchant lady of Thyatira, apparently devout, well-to-do, and hospitable. At Philippi there was a women's prayer group meeting outside the gate by the river side, and Paul thought it worth while to go there to meet with them. Lydia responded warmly as he spoke to them, was baptized with her household, and invited Paul (apparently Luke also as the narrator of the story) to make her home their headquarters. "And she prevailed upon us" (Acts 16:15) is a vivid understatement! Lydia's hospitality seems to have enabled Paul to stay for a time in Philippi without having to earn his living, as he usually had to elsewhere, and the notes of special fondness for the Philippian church in his letter to them from imprisonment in Rome may be related to this fact (Phil. 1:3-8; 4:1, 14-18).[3] After the imprisonment of Paul and Silas at Philippi and their miraculous release, they went back to see Lydia again before leaving the city (Acts 16:40). This little vignette shows us a woman energetic enough to have her own business in a day when few women did, able also to maintain a household, and concerned enough about her religion to worship and to serve.

And there was Dorcas, or Tabitha, a charitable woman of Joppa who was so full of good works that she was greatly mourned upon her death (Acts 9:36-43). The story tells us that at Peter's intercession she was miraculously restored to life, an element in the narrative which Luke apparently took from an early tradition in the Palestinian church. Be that as it may, it is worth pointing out that Dorcas is called a disciple, and that this is the only place in the New Testament where the feminine form of this word is used.[4]

Yet there was many a "discipless," if such an awkward term may be coined, throughout the churches. In Philippi we hear not only of Lydia but of Euodia and Syntyche. The two seem to have been dedicated Christian workers who could not agree with each other—no unusual phenomenon in Christian history! As Paul, writing from a Roman dungeon shortly before his death, penned immortal words to the Philippian church, he seems to have had them on his mind. Interspersed between great injunctions to courage and to joy and peace in the Lord we find him saying, "I entreat Euodia and I entreat Syntyche to agree in the Lord. And I ask you also, true yokefellow, help these women, for they have labored side by side with me in the gospel . . ." (Phil. 4:2-3). Irrelevant? Not if we remember that to Paul individuals mattered, and in paying tribute to his women fellow workers, he was unstinting in his appreciation.

There were other women among Paul's esteemed friends and coworkers about whom we know so little that we are apt to overlook them. Among these was Apphia. The lovely letter of Paul to Philemon in behalf of the slave Onesimus who had served Paul as a son during his imprisonment begins with the words, "To Philemon our beloved fellow worker and Apphia our sister and Archippus our fellow soldier, and the church in your house." Apphia may have been the wife of Philemon who presided over their home and its house church, or simply a sister in that Christian fellowship as the men were brothers. Anyway, Paul esteemed her highly.

Another woman of whom we know nothing except that Paul appreciated her was Nympha. In the closing words of his letter to the Colossian church we find this message (Col. 4:15), "Give my greetings to the brethren at Laodicea, and to Nympha and the church in her house." Probably she was a single woman or widow who was able and willing to have the church in her house, for no husband is mentioned.

However, it is in the last chapter of Romans, in Paul's letter of greeting to his many friends in that city, that we find the clearest evidence of his esteem for individual Christian women. This merits careful attention.

In Romans 16, twenty-eight individuals are mentioned, most of them otherwise unknown but thus immortalized. Their fidelity in Christian work had won Paul's affection and gratitude. Of this number nine are women, an astonishingly high proportion in view of prevailing social patterns and, we may add parenthetically, a higher proportion than is often found today in major ecclesiastical assemblies.

The list begins with "our sister Phoebe, a deaconess of the church at Cenchreae," a seaport community a few miles from Corinth. She was apparently entrusted with carrying the letter to Rome, for Paul commends her to its recipients and asks "that you may receive her in the Lord as befits the saints, and help her in whatever she may require from you, for she has been a helper of many and of myself as well" (Rom. 16:1-2). From this we learn that there were already special women workers called deaconesses, at whose duties we shall look in the next section. Then follows Paul's tribute to Priscilla and Aquila, previously noted. This suggests that by this time they had returned to Rome, their former residence, and doubtless were as active in the church there as they had been in Corinth and Ephesus. Briefer tributes to other women follow. "Greet Mary, who has worked hard among you" (vs. 6). "Greet those workers in the Lord, Tryphaena and Tryphosa. Greet the beloved Persis, who has worked hard in the Lord. Greet Rufus, eminent in the Lord, also his mother and mine (vss. 12-13). "Greet Philologus, Julia, Nereus and his sister, and Olympas, and all the saints who are with them. Greet one another with a holy kiss" (vss. 15-16).

In this outpouring of Paul's loving concern for both his male and female friends, doubtless all of whom had "worked hard in the Lord," there is no hint of condescension toward women or of a desire to subordinate or silence them. Apparently he not only accepted but encouraged and warmly appreciated the women of the churches. Such words as have been quoted cohere completely with the magnificent statement of racial, cultural, and sex equality in Christ which we find in his letter to the Galatian church:

For in Christ Jesus you are all sons of God, through faith. For as many of you as were baptized into Christ have put on Christ. There is neither Jew nor Greek, there is neither slave nor free, there is neither male nor female; for you are all one in Christ Jesus. (Gal. 3:26-28.)

But now we must look at those ugly words in which Paul tells women to look up to their husbands as Lord and Master, even as the men must look up to Christ; keep their heads covered in church; keep silent in the churches; and, if they wish to know anything, ask their husbands at home. There are two such passages in I Corinthians, a similar one in Ephesians of which the authorship is in dispute, and one in I Timothy which was written much later than Paul's time but was doubtless influenced by these other passages. They have been quoted times without number as evidence that "the Bible says" women must remain subordinate and silent in the churches.

Together, these passages make a formidable barrage against women's self-expression or leadership, in the church or elsewhere. So let us assemble them.

But I want you to understand that the head of every man is Christ, the head of a woman is her husband, and the head of Christ is God. Any man who prays or prophesies with his head covered dishonors his head, but any woman who prays or prophesies with her head unveiled dishonors her head— it is the same as if her head were shaven. . . . For a man ought not to cover his head, since he is the image and glory of God; but woman is the glory of man. (For man was not made from woman, but woman from man. Neither was man created for woman, but woman for man.) (I Cor. 11:3-9.)

As in all the churches of the saints, the women should keep silence in the churches. For they are not permitted to speak, but should be subordinate, as even the law says. If there is anything they desire to know, let them ask their husbands at home. For it is shameful for a woman to speak in church. (I Cor. 14:33-35.)

Wives, be subject to your husbands, as to the Lord. For the husband is the head of the wife as Christ is the head of the church, his body, and is himself its Savior. As the church is subject to Christ, so let wives also be subject in everything to their husbands. (Eph. 5:22-24.)

Let a woman learn in silence with all submissiveness. I permit no woman to teach or to have authority over men; she is to keep silent. For Adam was formed first, then Eve; and Adam was not deceived, but the woman was deceived and became a transgressor. (I Tim. 2:11-14.)

Immediately preceding the last passage, women are told not to adorn themselves with gold or pearls or costly attire—an injunction few biblical literalists expect to see carried out—and if women were debarred from teaching in the churches today, the Sunday schools would have a hard time to muster a staff.

Whatever may be thought of the last two passages, the first two appear to be from Paul's hand. Why did he say such things?

The question is far more than an academic one, for these passages are known and quoted a hundred times to one over the other passages in which Paul shows a fine appreciation of his women friends and coworkers. They have doomed women to subordination and exclusion from leadership in both church and society, and even today their effects are felt. In renouncing the Bible as a guide the secular world may smile at these passages, but indirectly their effects remain in almost every form of social relationship. In ecclesiastical circles they are quoted repeatedly, especially in regard to the ordination of women, and even among those who have broken with biblical literalism they remain as an unconscious conditioning.

Before attempting to say how a person of such intellectual strength and acumen as Paul could say such contradictory things about women, another internal problem must be looked at. Paul *did* permit women to speak in the services of worship. How do we know? Because he says in I Corinthians 11:5 in the midst of his strictures, "any woman who prays or prophesies with her head unveiled dishonors her head." We noted that from the earliest days of the church, women as well as men took part in "the breaking of bread and the prayers" (Acts 2:42), and there is no indication that this practice ceased. Less is said about prophesying, which probably does not mean preaching in a formal sense but "speaking in meeting," whether with or without the speaking in tongues. However, we are told in Acts 21:9 that Philip the evangelist had four unmarried daughters who prophesied. But to come back to Paul, why should he have been so explicit about what women should wear when they prophesied if they were not to prophesy at all?

Attempts have been made to resolve this contradiction by holding that I Cor. 14:34-35 originated as a marginal gloss inserted later by another hand, or by the inference that I Cor. 11:3-9 presupposes the greater freedom of the small house congregation. However, other possibilities are open.

The answer to the conundrum is partially found in the presence of the hetaerae of shady reputation in the wicked, wealthy city of Corinth, and Paul's eagerness not to have the Christian women confused with them. But this does not tell the whole story. We must look deeper for an explanation.

I believe the explanation is to be found in Paul's total background, not all of which was changed by his dramatic conversion. Then as now, "if any one is in Christ, he is a new creation" (II Cor. 5:17). But never wholly new. Social conditionings from childhood may remain, and in one's subconscious depths prejudices die hard. We see this clearly in the contemporary Christian and his racial attitudes as an illustration.

Paul was a Jew, a Pharisee and a son of Pharisees (Acts 23:6). Of his earlier years he says in his defense before Agrippa, "According to the strictest party of our religion I have lived as a Pharisee" (Acts 26:5). All that did not change on the Damascus Road! Much did, and the change accounts for his warm appreciation of women workers in the church and the great Christian insight of his words in Galatians 3:28. Yet centuries of inherited belief in the inherent inferiority of women and therefore their necessary subordination to men remained. There was the early Genesis story which Paul quotes, and which no biblical scholar had yet demonstrated to be meaningful myth rather than historic fact. But there was also the whole Old Testament and centuries of Jewish living. No wonder Paul remained a Jew in some aspects of his outlook, the indelible product not only of his immediate environment but of a long past.

Of individual women, Paul could speak highly and gratefully and feel with them a fine fellowship in Christ. But of the man-woman relation, he spoke his inherited rather than his Christian conviction when he said that as the head of man is Christ, so the head of a woman is her husband, and that man is the image and glory of God while woman is the glory of man.

And if this be so, let the women keep still and the men do the talking!

I believe this to be the explanation because I have seen it demonstrated so often in my own long experience in church circles. I cannot recall an occasion when a Christian man has treated me disrespectfully. Many women like myself who have worked actively in the churches have received from men fine treatment as individuals. Yet repeatedly I have sat in male-dominated assemblies in which most of the men present had no idea of the extent to which they were violating Paul's word, "for as many among you as were baptized into Christ have put on Christ. . . . There is neither male nor female; for you are all one in Christ Jesus." When women have attempted to take some steps, albeit modest ones, toward greater equality in church life, there were smiles which grew to snickers, then outright laughter.[5] Often there seemed to be complete oblivion in the male contingent that anything needed to be done. Yet sometimes, let it be said in fairness to all, a woman has "prophesied" so effectively that the men applauded!

3. *Deaconess, widow, and virgin*

We must now move more rapidly over the later centuries in which the subordination of women was tightened, then held in this restriction with almost unbroken continuity to the modern period.

There were three "orders" of women in the early church, if that term is not given too ecclesiastical a connotation. Deaconesses, widows, and virgins are referred to briefly in the New Testament and in subsequent writings, but so little is said of their duties that we are left with many unanswered questions. In fact, much of our knowledge comes from statements of what they were prohibited from doing, or could do only in a subordinate capacity.

In the New Testament the one specific reference to deaconesses is to Phoebe in Romans 16:1-2. However, there may be an indirect reference in I Timothy 3:11. Interjected between statements of the qualifications of deacons are these words: "The women likewise must be serious, no slanderers, but temperate, faithful in all things." Does this mean the wives of deacons, as the King James version has it,[6] or women church workers with duties comparable to those of deacons as these are outlined in Acts 6? We are left in doubt and are informed only of their qualifications of character, not their duties or status.

Apparently a deaconess might carry the sacraments to the sick, for Justin Martyr in the second century says that in doing this she is an assistant to the bishop, not a minister of the altar.[7] The fullest original statement we have of the duties and status of the deaconess is in the Syrian *Didascalia Apostolorum* from about the year 300, which pays her a high tribute:

The bishop sits for you in the place of Almighty God. But the deacon stands in the place of Christ: and you do love him. And the deaconess shall be honored by you in the place of the Holy Spirit; and the presbyters shall be to you in the likeness of Apostles; and the orphans and widows shall be reckoned by you in the likeness of the altar.[8]

This same document also indicates that the deaconess may prepare women for baptism, go down with them into the water and anoint them, but may not pronounce the baptismal formula. The reason given is the somewhat lame one, though no lamer than some in our time for denying women the administering of the sacraments, that if it were lawful for a woman to baptize, Jesus should have been baptized by his mother rather than by John. But the document indicates important things for the deaconess to do—she is to visit in the homes of unbelievers where there are believing women, distribute charity, visit the sick, and bathe those recovering from illness.

Were deaconesses ever ordained, and thus given official standing in the churches? The best answer we have to this question, and it is still an ambiguous one, is from the *Apostolic Constitutions* in the later fourth century. This document provides for the ordination of both deacons and deaconesses by the laying on of hands, but with a significant difference. The prayer for the men is that they may serve faithfully and thus be "appointed eventually to higher office in the church"; the prayer for the woman is that God will "grant her the Holy Spirit . . . that she may worthily accomplish the work committed to her." [9] Since the church had as yet no monolithic structure, the practice seems to have differed in different places. Ambrose in the fourth century says that women are not allowed to hold office in the church, while his contemporary Jerome says that they do in the East.

There was a sociological reason for this difference in practice between the churches of the East and West. Where women were by custom segregated and confined to their own quarters, female visitors were needed, for it would have caused embarrassment if not scandal for a male clergyman to visit them in these quarters. This situation prevailed in the East, but in the West the social conventions permitted much greater freedom.

There is some doubt about the ordination of deaconesses in the Western church, but there seems little doubt that they were ordained in the Eastern. But this does not mean that they were given the full authority of the male diaconate in either area. D. S. Bailey in his excellent *Sexual Relation in Christian Thought* summarizes succinctly with extensive references what they could and could not do:

The nature of their office was not limited by any acknowledged defect of order, but only by a restriction of function due to sex. Thus their ministry was almost exclusively a ministry to women; they acted as intermediaries between them and the bishop, they assisted them at baptism, visited them when sick, and taught them, besides serving as doorkeepers at the church entrances reserved for females. But they remained subject none the less to the same ecclesiastical disabilities as the rest of their sex. A woman might not offer the oblations nor perform any duty properly belonging to a male, she might not baptize (even in cases of necessity), she might not teach in church or in assemblies of men, regardless of her learning or holiness, she might not pray aloud in church, approach the altar, or pronounce a blessing.[10]

Bailey adds also that these restrictions are in sharp contrast to the practices in some of the heretical sects, where women played a much more active part. It will be recalled that among the Montanists, Maximilla and Priscilla were regarded as original prophetesses of the sect, almost equal in authority to Montanus himself, but by the authority of the Holy Spirit rather than an ecclesiastical Council.

We must turn now to the second of the female "orders" in the early church, the widows. Of these we are told more in the New Testament than of

75

deaconesses. In I Timothy 5:3-16 the author speaks of widows and "real widows," probably those whose husbands had died and left them without support. The church felt responsible for them but in turn expected some service. However, there were other "widows" performing similar functions, who might even be unmarried women. The author of the letter wants all widows enrolled by the church to be at least sixty years of age, for he fears the younger ones may be indiscreet gad-abouts looking for a husband and making trouble rather than being real servants of Christ. They had better marry!

In spite of this longer biblical reference, we know less about widows than about deaconesses. They seem to have had few duties except prayer, though in some places they engaged in charitable works and in ministry to the sick. Ignatius refers to them as "intercessors of the church," and sends greetings to those in Smyrna, to whom he refers as "the maidens who are called widows." [11] The passage in I Timothy referring to young widows who gossip as they go from house to house may indicate parish visitors. There is no indication that widows ever constituted an order in the church to the extent of the deaconesses, or had even their quasi-ordination.

The third group of women set apart for the service of the Lord were the virgins. As indicated earlier, Philip had four virgin daughters who prophesied. Probably not all the virgin group prophesied, or we should have heard more about them. Paul confesses that he has no command from the Lord about virgins (I Cor. 7:25). He then goes on to state an "interim ethic" about marital matters which shows that he expected the end of the world to be coming soon. He may have had in mind those who had taken special vows of celibacy, but the context suggests that he was speaking of the unmarried of both sexes.

Apparently some did take such vows, but this did not constitute a sacerdotal office.[12] When the Church Fathers said anything about them, it was mainly over whether they should be veiled in church according to the Pauline injunction. Some of them apparently did not wish to be thus limited. Tertullian wrote a strong invective against any such freedom in a treatise entitled, *On the Veiling of Women,* and in it took the occasion to make numerous uncomplimentary references to women in any kind of "manly function."

Even the usually gentle-spirited Clement of Alexandria wrote words more relevant to the present day than he could possibly have imagined when he said, "For neither is it seemly for clothes to be above the knee, as they say was the case with the Lacedaemonian virgins; nor is it becoming for any part of a woman to be exposed." [13]

Whether deaconess, widow, or virgin, these special offices for women within the churches died out in a few centuries. Aspirants were "put in their place" repeatedly by the Church Fathers. All in all, not one of these showed the degree of appreciation of the services of women that Paul did, and some were vitriolic. The severe words of Paul had much quoting, and these in conjunction with other social pressures put an end to any "women's liberation movement" that might have ensued from the spirit of Jesus or the magnanimous side of Paul. Not until the conventual movement as an adjunct to monasticism do women reappear in any position of honor.

4. *The middle centuries*

In this section we shall look rapidly, not at the Middle Ages in the usual meaning of the term, but at the longer sweep of history from the end of the period of the Church Fathers to the nineteenth century. Our main concern will be those developments affecting the status of women which have left an influence into the present.

One of these developments was the increase of asceticism in the mores of the church, and with it the acceptance of celibacy as a higher status than marriage. This had a strong influence on sexual morality, in some respects constructive but in others unhealthy.

There was nothing ascetic about Jesus in his view either of sex or the normal pleasures of life. He did enjoin a strict monogamy, and taught that life is more than food and the body than raiment, but one has to strain the record considerably to make an ascetic out of Jesus. Paul has much to say about sexual impurity, and his blunt "It is better to marry than to be aflame with passion" (I Cor. 7:9) falls considerably short of accenting the spiritual aspects of married love. But neither in the words of Jesus nor those of Paul is celibacy the norm for servants of the church, though both make it a live option.

Gradually, however, the idea that the sexual impulse is inherently evil came to be embedded in Christian thinking. Along with other considerations the natural result was a celibate priesthood. This issue is not the central concern of this book, though the protest within the Catholic Church of today against papal restrictions on both birth control and the marriage of priests has a common rootage with the Women's Liberation Movement.

But what of the relation of ascetic ideas of Christian sexual morality to women? This cut in two directions. One of these was to accent the sinfulness of woman as the temptress. Any illicit sexual union was viewed as the woman's fault. Had there been no Héloise, Abelard's life could have run a smooth and uninterrupted course. In many a less famous liaison the woman took the brunt of it, not only by her pregnancy but in popular disfavor. A double standard of morality was established which has not yet been eradicated.

The constructive side of Christian sex morals was an emphasis on fidelity in marriage, an aversion to obscenity, the need of sexual self-control and self-discipline. This is often disparaged today as Puritan or Victorian, but insofar as these terms are synonyms for sexual purity and decency they ought not to be pejorative.

However, even purity in sex morals had some unhealthy fruits when divorced from the love commandment and spirit of Jesus. Christians forgot his word spoken to the woman taken in adultery, "Neither do I condemn you; go, and do not sin again." As a result, the sexual deviant came to be despised. The male offender could cover his tracks, but the prostitute, the adulteress, or the homosexual of either sex became not a person beloved of God but a social outcast. The extent to which this is still true among "respectable" Christians needs no documentation.

Another unhealthy fruit was the sanctioning of unlimited freedom in sexuality within marriage. As a result large families, limited only by high rates of infant mortality, became the social pattern. What this did in adding to the burdens of women requires no elaboration. It is enough to say that it is directly related to problems of population control, contraceptives, abortion, and day care centers for the employed woman in today's world.

Another large issue, related to the preceding but from a different angle, was the increasing veneration of the Virgin Mary. Addressed repeatedly in prayer as "mother of God" and viewed with great devotion as Mediatrix and Co-Redeemer, she assumed a position in the church which has often been compared with that of the great mother-goddess so commonly found in pre-Christian religions. In any event, her veneration as primary intercessor for the faithful lifted high the feminine principle in regard to deity. But did this lift the position of the ordinary earthbound woman? There is no evidence that it did. Virginity was required of one professing a religious vocation, whether male or female. But for the married woman, sexual intercourse was solely for the procreation of children, and there must be no interruption of the course of nature viewed as the will and work of God.

To turn to a brighter side of what was happening to the role of women in the middle centuries, we must look at monasticism. Initially this was a male movement, but very early there began to be monastic groups for women. Marcella, a friend of Jerome in the late fourth century, is credited with being the first woman to organize such a group in her own home. When Benedict of Nursia established the famous and influential Benedictine order at Monte Cassino about 530, his sister Scholastica established one for women at the foot of the mountain. From that time to the present there have been both male and female monasteries, the latter often called convents to distinguish them.

It is well known that monasteries were of great importance before and during the Middle Ages because of their educational and other services, and in an unsettled time they did much to preserve not only religion and learning but social stability. But our concern here is what they did for the status of women.

Though the results varied from one convent or one order to another, they were on the whole a very constructive force. Here a woman could have the religious vocation denied her in other forms of church life. Here she could have security, dignity, and usually a satisfying social life among her peers. Here she could study, learn, and teach, and sometimes have a high order of cultural life, for the times, in art, music, drama, or literature. Here she would have work to do, but also time for meditation. Unless it were a cloistered order withdrawn from the world, as some became, she could go out into the world to serve the poor, the sick, and the suffering. Famous among these was the work of the Poor Clares, founded by the Lady Clare of Assisi, whose ministry continues to the present as the Second Order of St. Francis.

Such monasteries were usually presided over by an abbess. Some abbesses exercised great administrative authority, not only over their own domains but over the double monasteries where monks and nuns lived in adjacent communities. In the tenth century and thereafter, there were those who wielded much power in the affairs of both church and state. It was the castle courtyard (not the cloister) of Matilda of Tuscany at Canossa, while Pope Gregory VII was a guest, where King Henry

IV stood barefoot in the snow for three days to entreat the Pope to absolve him from excommunication.

In the middle centuries the convents nourished also the great women mystics, the greatest of whom was St. Teresa of Avila, a Spanish mystic of the sixteenth century. She was a remarkable woman, not only in the depth of her spiritual insights and the intellectual acumen of her writing, but in her tireless labors for the spiritual life of the church and the reform of her Carmelite order of nuns. We should add to the list Juliana of Norwich, St. Catherine of Siena, St. Catherine of Genoa, and numerous others.

Whether monastic life for men or women is appropriate to the conditions of the present is a matter of difference of opinion and of an individual sense of vocation. Yet conventual life in the middle centuries gave women a status and opportunity for personhood not available elsewhere. The vows of poverty, chastity, and obedience, illumined with a sense of religious calling, may well have seemed less constricting than the humdrum society, wifely submission. and overburdened child-bearing of their contemporaries.

But was there not much chivalry in those days "when knighthood was in flower"? A knight must be polite and gracious to the lady he loved, and must fight bravely in her defense or to win her favor against his rivals. Indeed, a true knight must come to the rescue of any lady in distress. It is well that some aspects of chivalry have persisted to the present. But such chivalry was oblivious to the burdens of women unless the distress was overt enough to be dramatically visible. The burden of being a nonentity and a drudge was bypassed. Furthermore, chivalry was rooted in the assumption of the inferiority and helplessness of women. Monasticism in the middle centuries was the Christian woman's one breakthrough to something like the opportunities and privileges of men. If that is not appropriate to the present scene, another course must be found, for chivalry however commendable will not suffice.

With the Protestant Reformation came important changes in ecclesiastical structure and belief. Some of these affected the status of women, though less than might have been expected from the Protestant emphasis on individual liberty before God and the sacredness of the common life. Priestly celibacy was renounced by Protestant clergy. Some monks and nuns left their monasteries to marry. As Protestantism became a political force, many monasteries were closed and their lands taken over by the State. This was a setback for women. It deprived the nuns of their former privileges, and it robbed many girls who had formerly been taught by them of an education. In the seventeenth century some Baptist and Quaker women, less ecclesiastically trammeled than in the other churches, began to preach, but in general the restrictions on the preaching or other public ministry of women continued. While these events were taking place, the status of the ordinary woman in her household changed very little.

Neither Luther nor Calvin gave a thought to the equality of women as persons. Their marriages give evidence of this fact. Both married to prove to the world that the celibacy of the priesthood must be abandoned. Luther married an ex-nun who had no other provision available, and wrote to a friend that he "had stopped the mouths of his calumniators with Katherine von Bora." This resulted in a happy marriage and a large family, but though loving them all deeply he ruled the household. Calvin thought he ought to marry, not only to show that he repudiated celibacy, but to have some one to free him from many cares so that he could devote himself fully to the Lord's work. He wrote to his colleague Farel that he would be interested only in "a woman who is chaste, agreeable, modest, frugal, patient, and affords me some hope that she will be solicituous for my personal health and prosperity." Such a wife was found, and after her early death he paid her the high compliment of saying that she had never in any way interfered with his work.[14]

Meanwhile the typical Protestant woman, like the Catholic, went on marrying, submitting to her husband's wishes, bearing many children, losing many of them, and having her own strength sapped and health endangered in the process. The Protestant exaltation of the Bible as the infallible Word of God accentuated this process, for was it not written in the Bible that "the head of every man is Christ, and the head of a woman is her husband"?

Some strong women emerged, both queens and housewives. Susannah Wesley is an example of the latter who has made a place for herself in history, a woman of remarkable ability, well educated for her time, and superlative in the rearing of her children. However, she was obliged to bear nineteen children, losing nine of them. John Wesley and his brother Charles were the seventeenth and eighteenth of this brood, and the questionable argument sometimes used is that there must be no birth control, since it might prevent the birth of persons of such genius late in the succession. The production of nineteen children, or any major fraction thereof, from two parents can today hardly be held compatible with the conditions of the good life for all upon our crowded planet.

84

There were other women of distinction, both before and after Susannah Wesley, who have left their mark on history. There was Anne Hutchinson, independent spirit in the midst of New England Calvinism, who disliked its theological rigidity and advocated a covenant of grace instead of works, with a direct approach to God through the Holy Spirit rather than the ecclesiastical authorities. Banished from Boston and "delivered up to Satan" under a horrible indictment, she and her followers withdrew to Rhode Island and there helped to lay the foundations of religious liberty.

That was in the mid-1600s. Almost two centuries later, Elizabeth Fry, an English Quaker preacher, became so stirred by the deplorable conditions in the British prisons for women that she felt she must speak out in protest. Some other Quakers joined her, and the result was more tolerable treatment, first for the women imprisoned at Newgate, then in the ships carrying convicts to Australia, and eventually in other prisons. Such assertions of woman power were luminous but rare.

Thus it came about that a long-embedded paternalism, ecclesiastical restrictions, biblical literalism, Pauline prohibitions, and the pull of all these in combination within the social structure denied to women for centuries their human identity and equality as persons. In the nineteenth century, the hard shell of custom began to crack. At this movement we must now look.

IV The modern woman appears

In the preceding chapters we have surveyed the subordinate status of women from primitive times up to the nineteenth century. Since the first eighteen centuries of the Christian era were largely dominated in the Western World by the church and a literal understanding of the Bible, much of the previous chapter centers at that point. With the coming of the nineteenth century and the stirring of new life in many directions, including the rights and opportunities of women, we move into a somewhat different setting. Some of the women who began to disturb the ancient mores were preachers; many more were committed Christians who felt impelled by their faith to speak out against slavery, intemperance, war, and the denial to women of the right to vote and to determine their destiny as persons. Some few had no special religious motivation, and since the movement on the whole was socially rather than ecclesiastically based, it is impossible to judge precisely to what extent religion figured in it. It is clear that the secularization so prominent in the present Women's Liberation Movement was not characteristic of the nineteenth-century stirrings.[1]

1. *Beginnings*

We must begin by looking a little back of the nineteenth century, toward the end of the eighteenth. Here we find some remarkable words by a remarkable woman, Abigail Adams, the wife of the second President of the United States and mother of the sixth. During her husband's long absences in Congress and elsewhere she wrote him letters which have fortunately been preserved. In 1777 she penned this epistle: "In the new code of laws which I suppose it will be necessary for you to make, I desire you would remember the ladies and be more generous and favorable to them than your ancestors. . . . If particular care and attention is not paid to the ladies, we are determined to foment a rebellion, and will not hold ourselves bound by any laws in which we have no voice or representation." [2]

Abigail Adams herself did not "foment a rebellion," but one was in the making. During the 1780s Judith Murray, about whom little seems to be known except her name and a vital concern, was appealing for better education for girls, domesticated from their earliest years while large opportunities were open to their brothers. She put it bluntly in these words: "Is it reasonable that a candidate for immortality, for the joys of heaven, an intelligent being, who is to spend an eternity contemplating the works of Deity . . . should be . . . allowed no other ideas, than those which are suggested by the mechanism of a pudding?" [3]

The person most often credited with launching the woman's movement was Mary Wollstonecraft, an English woman who in 1792 published her *Vindication of the Rights of Women*. In it she stated a truism which now seems evident to many women, though perhaps to fewer men: "Men, in general, seem to employ their reason to justify prejudices, which they have imbibed, they cannot trace how, rather than root them out." [4] She was a married woman, at first self-educated and then in touch with the Enlightenment philosophy of her time. Simone de Beauvoir in her monumental work, *The Second Sex,* says that this effort of Mary Wollstonecraft's was largely abortive because the Industrial Revolution was not yet far enough advanced to give women a measure of independence in the world of work outside the home.[5]

The economic factor was bound to increase in importance, and in the twentieth century to become a very vital factor in the quest of women for a new freedom. But for the early nineteenth, Judith Murray had hit the nail on the head. After the turn of the century it was in the advent of fresh opportunities for the education of women that the primary foundations were laid for the rise of a protest movement. Three famous educators of this era, who spearheaded the opening of the "female seminaries," merit special attention. These are Emma Willard (1787-1870), Mary Lyon (1797-1849), and Catherine Beecher (1800-1878).

From the earliest days in America there were sporadic attempts to give girls some elementary education in the three R's in the village "dame schools," and after the Revolutionary War the town schools of New England were opened to them. But beyond this, scarcely anything was available except the boarding schools or "finishing schools" for those whose parents could afford it. Imported from England, these gave little instruction except in "female accomplishments" such as dancing, piano playing, and art work in yarns or paints. They were geared toward fitting a girl to secure a husband and become the gracious mistress of her home. Any other goal was unthinkable for a self-respecting girl! The female seminaries, on the other hand, taught such masculine subjects as mathematics, history, geography, literature, Latin, and at least a smattering of book science. No wonder they and their founders were frowned upon! All three of the pioneer women we shall discuss saw the need to educate women, not only to be intelligent wives and mothers, but to be teachers in the public schools and to be well-informed persons in their own selfhood.

The first of the three to become active in the education of women was Emma Hart Willard, who in 1905, thirty-five years after her death, was elected to the Hall of Fame. In 1819 she published her famous "Address . . . to the Members of the Legislature of New York Proposing a Plan for Female Education," an address that was printed in pamphlet form because she was not permitted to deliver it in person. In it she declared that "female education has been left to the mercy of private adventurers," and that the girls' schools of that day were "temporary institutions, formed by individuals, whose object is present emolument." As a result the schools were adequate neither in accommodations nor in the type of instruction being given. The cause of these defects, she said, was the undervaluing by legislatures of the importance of women in society.

In this appeal she had the support of Governor Clinton. Whether through her persuasiveness or his influence, she secured an act of incorporation and a small allocation of funds to establish a "female seminary" at Waterford, N.Y. This was a historic step, the first such move by any legislature to provide directly for the education of women. However, the funds were presently abruptly withdrawn by the Regents of the State University. This was a keen disappointment, but after some persuasion the school was moved to Troy, N.Y. in 1821 by invitation of its citizens. As the Troy Female Seminary it then furnished the inspiration for many other such seminaries, said to have been nearly two hundred.[6] As the Emma Willard School it still exists in full vigor after a century and a half of changing times.

A younger contemporary of Mrs. Willard, Mary Lyon, was less of an innovator but has the distinction of having established at South Hadley, Mass. in 1837 a female seminary which was to become one of the great woman's colleges of today. I taught for a time at Mount Holyoke College, and as I passed her grave on the campus near the original building I read repeatedly the inscription which epitomizes the determination of her life: "There is nothing in the universe that I fear, but that I shall not know all my duty, or shall fail to do it." This seminary was from the start privately financed, first by the help of a few gentlemen who had confidence in Mary Lyon and her ideas, then by her own efforts as she traveled about soliciting subscriptions to furnish the first building. The whole project met with much opposition and ridicule, but determination won. Firm foundations of both intellectual and religious culture were laid, and the influence of the school through many decades has spread throughout the world.

The third member of the trio was Catherine Beecher. She was the daughter of Lyman Beecher, famous New England preacher and theologian, and was the older sister of Harriet Beecher Stowe of *Uncle Tom's Cabin* fame and the Brooklyn preacher Henry Ward Beecher. In 1822 she opened what became a celebrated school at Hartford, Conn. Like Mrs. Willard,[7] she was deeply concerned with the training of teachers and wrote some textbooks. She even ventured in her writing into the field of theology—certainly for her time an unusual pursuit for a woman to regard as her province. Mrs.

Phebe Hanaford in *Daughters of America* says of Catherine Beecher: "For the sake of her own pupils, she prepared her first printed work on Arithmetic. Her second work was on the more difficult points of Theology; and her third, an octavo, on Mental and Moral Philosophy." [8]

But what of the college education of women in those days? Here the story is mixed, and one must be cautious in claims that one institution or another is the earliest. Oberlin College, founded as the Oberlin Collegiate Institute in 1833, was from the beginning coeducational, and thus the first to admit women. But it had a diluted and abridged "ladies' course" as an alternate to the course leading to a college degree, and this is what most of its woman students took. Some, like Antoinette Brown and Lucy Stone of whom we shall speak presently, did take the college course, but Antoinette found rock-ribbed opposition when she wished to move from this to work in the divinity school.

Georgia Female College, now Wesleyan College, was chartered by the Georgia State Legislature in 1836. Its first class entered in January, 1839. Mount Holyoke College opened as a female seminary in 1837, but was not called a college until 1888. Elmira College, founded in 1855, had a curriculum "equivalent to that of the best men's colleges of the time." But it lacked money, and the first heavily endowed woman's college was Vassar, which opened its doors in 1865 and thus claims to be "the oldest of the well equipped and amply endowed colleges for women in the United States."

Which, then, is the oldest of the woman's colleges? One has to define the ground of the claim in order to make it. It happens that I have taught in two of these "oldest woman's colleges," and thus have come to see the need of getting the formula straight. Perhaps it is better to say simply that all four of them are institutions of enduring excellence which paved the way for the emergence of women to greater service and freedom in the mid-nineteenth century.

Such institutions contributed directly to the women's movement by educating many of its ablest leaders. But as precursors of the later state-supported normal schools, they also made available an adequate supply of well-trained teachers for the public schools. Salaries were pitifully small—usually one fourth to one half of what men received—but teaching became an honorable profession for women, and the general level of education for both boys and girls was in process of being lifted.

In this early period there also were literary figures who merit more space than we can give them. Hannah Adams (1755-1832), largely self-educated, left off making lace for a living in order to help prepare young men for college. She wrote a number of books. Among these were *The View of Religions* (a summary of the Christian denominations and the religions of the world), *The History of the Jews,* and *The Evidences of the Christian Religion.* She also formed a woman's club in 1818, perhaps the first of its kind.

Sarah Josepha Hale (1788-1879), is believed to have written the immortal "Mary had a little lamb." Many today are familiar with the Godey prints, but few know that Sarah Hale was the editor of the widely read (and profitable) *Godey's Lady's Book.* She was the author of at least ten books, of which her *Woman's Record* has preserved information about many women who would otherwise today be forgotten. She also compiled *A Complete Dictionary of Poetical Quotations,* a kind of pre-

Bartlett compendium of 600 double-column octavo pages.

Lydia Maria Child (1802-1880) wrote both prose and poetry. Her *Appeal for That Class of Americans Called Africans* was the first book on slavery to be published in the United States. It brought her both fame and ostracism. With her husband, David Lee Child, she edited the *Anti-Slavery Standard.* She edited also an "Anti-Slavery Almanac" and published an "Anti-Slavery Catechism." [9] For many years she used her pen with great effectiveness.

Let no one say there were not great women in those days! But meanwhile the ordinary woman in the ordinary home was baking the family bread and pastry, knitting hose for the family and making their garments, which often included those of the boys and men, weaving wool and flax (I have inherited some of their blankets and linens), piecing patchwork quilts, making soap, molding candles, churning the butter, salting down the meat. And all the while—bearing children. There was a kind of greatness in the courage and skill with which they did these things. But there was hardship also, for with all the chores to be done in the house, the women were still expected at times to help the menfolks in the barns and fields. Mrs. Stone milked eight cows the night before Lucy was born to her and on being told that the new baby was a girl, she said, "I'm so sorry it is a girl. A woman's life is so hard!"

Movements were stirring which were to challenge woman's subordination at its roots.

2. *Women's rights—London and Seneca Falls*

None of these moves, not the higher education of women nor their new role in literature, tackled directly the legal and civil rights of women. Even in the field of woman's education—now so taken for granted that we are apt to forget it was ever new—there was plenty of opposition and ridicule, and when women began to write books they were jeered at as unsexed, rather than admired. But with the enlargement of social vision, particularly on slavery and strong drink, on the part of a growing number of women, and with the sharpening of skills in public speaking along with ideas to talk about, something was bound to happen.

The two women who did most to inaugurate the new movement were Elizabeth Cady Stanton (1816-1902) and Lucretia Collins Mott (1793-1880) who first met at an abolitionist meeting in London in 1840. We must look therefore at the backgrounds of these women and the occasion of their meeting.

Elizabeth Cady was the daughter of Judge Daniel Cady of Johnstown, N.Y., and her education not only included attendance at the Troy Female Seminary but much familiarity with the cases which came before her father for settlement. Many of these had to do with a wife's earnings or inheritance, which a husband could invest, drink up, or squander at will, and with divorce or other domestic problems in which the wife had no legal redress. She came early to have a keen feeling of the need to change the laws in regard to intemperance, divorce and other domestic relations, slavery, and suffrage. Mutual interests led to her marriage to a young lawyer and opponent of slavery, Henry B. Stanton. He was a delegate to the World's Anti-Slavery Convention to be held in London in 1840, whence they went together on their honeymoon.

There she met Mrs. Lucretia Mott, a Quaker lady

of remarkable vigor and active Christian saintliness, and the two became lifelong friends. Mrs. Mott, feeling strongly the social imperatives of the Christian gospel "to preach deliverance to the captives" and "to set at liberty them that are bruised," had become a Quaker preacher. In this she was uninhibited in the Society of Friends by the kind of prejudice which would have prevented this course of action in the main line churches, though she was to confront external opposition for many years. The causes which had chiefly engaged her concern up to the time of the London meeting were temperance, peace, the oppression of the working classes,[10] and the slavery issue. She had spoken on these themes, particularly the last one, very frequently and, with seven other women, was made an official delegate to the London Conference.[11]

However, when they reached London the credentials of all the women delegates were rejected because they were women, and they had to sit it out in a gallery as listeners only. William Lloyd Garrison in indignation at this action elected to sit with them, and not to make the speech which had been expected from him.[12] Both Mrs. Mott and Mrs. Stanton were much disturbed by this discrimination, and Mrs. Mott puts it gently but unequivocally in these words, "This brought the woman question more into view; and an increase of interest in the subject has been the result." [13] Mrs. Stanton in her account of the incident adds a priceless touch about Mrs. Wendell Phillips, also a delegate but denied a seat on the floor of the Convention. "Her whole soul seemed to be in the pending issue. As we were about to enter the Convention, she laid her hand most emphatically on her husband's shoulder and said, 'Now, Wendell, don't be simmy-sammy today, but brave as a lion'; and he obeyed the injunction." [14]

We come now to the famous Seneca Falls Women's Rights Convention in 1848, of which Elizabeth Cady Stanton was the prime mover. It was she who called the Convention, made the arrangements, and wrote the "Declaration of Sentiments" which were adopted there and are still being quoted today.

The Stantons had moved to the small town of Seneca Falls in upstate New York. Elizabeth Stanton, though in fairly comfortable circumstances in the care of her young family, felt keenly both the legal restrictions and injustices of which she had learned from her father's office and the "hard life" of most women in the endless round of cooking, sewing, washing, and the bearing and rearing of each new child. Why should not women as well as men have a chance for cultural pursuits and the service of causes? So she secured the use of the Wesleyan Chapel and put a notice in the newspaper calling for a two-day meeting on July 19 and 20, 1848.

The response was overwhelming. People came in their wagons from fifty miles around, 300 of them of whom about forty were men, to discuss these issues and to hear Mrs. Lucretia Mott speak on the social, legal, and religious restrictions placed upon women. In deference to custom James Mott, Lucretia's husband, presided.

The platform of the Convention, adopted on its second day, begins with a deliberate paraphrase of the Declaration of Independence and moves gradually into the bearing of such independence on the rights of women.

We hold these truths to be self-evident: that all men and women are created equal; that they are endowed by their

Creator with certain inalienable rights; that among these are life, liberty, and the pursuit of happiness; that to secure these rights governments are instituted, deriving their just powers from the consent of the governed. . . . But when a long train of abuses and usurpations . . . evinces a design to reduce them under absolute despotism, it is their duty to throw off such government, and to provide new guards for their future security. Such has been the patient sufferance of the women under this government, and such is now the necessity which constrains them to demand the equal station to which they are entitled.

The history of mankind is a history of repeated injuries and usurpations on the part of man toward woman, having in direct object the establishment of an absolute tyranny over her. To prove this, let facts be submitted to a candid world.

The facts then submitted make up the body of the document and the most biting part of the Declaration. This is too long to quote in full,[15] but among its items are the denial of the elective franchise; the making of laws constraining women, granting them no voice; the withholding of rights given to the most ignorant and degraded men; the denial to the married woman of legal rights to property, even to the wages she earns; obedience to and submission to husbands in marriage; denial of the guardianship of children in divorce; the closing of avenues to college education and to service in the professions such as the ministry, theology, law, and medicine; a double standard of moral delinquencies.

The list of grievances ends with this indictment:

He has usurped the prerogative of Jehovah himself, claiming it as his right to assign for her a sphere of action, when that belongs to her conscience and to her God.

97

He has endeavored, in every way that he could, to destroy her confidence in her own powers, to lessen her self-respect, and to make her willing to lead a dependent and abject life.

The Declaration of Sentiments was adopted and with it twelve resolutions, all of them unanimously except one which read, "*Resolved,* That it is the duty of the women of this country to secure to themselves their sacred right to the elective franchise." Some thought this went too far! The document was signed by 68 women and 32 men, and the women's rights movement was on its way.

The event drew publicity almost equal to the California gold rush of the following year. The Seneca Falls Declaration produced such an outcry of insurrection and blasphemy that some of the more fainthearted withdrew their names. Then, as in a comparable movement of the present, it was met with incredulity and laughter by men who could not take it seriously. The attacks were especially virulent from the newspapers—though Horace Greeley of the *New York Tribune* gave it respectful attention—and from the clergy who could forthwith quote Saint Paul in opposition to it.

Yet the movement, now come to birth, was destined to live and to grow. It continued to meet with much opposition, but a new mood had been aroused which grew in power until in 1874—to anticipate a bit—the Rev. Leo Miller wrote a book entitled *Woman and the Divine Republic* as a theological defense of the woman's movement. In it he begins his first chapter with the words, "The civil and political enfranchisement of woman, at no distant day, is now pretty generally accepted as a foregone conclusion, both by intelligent opposers of the cause as well as by its friends." [16]

3. *The movement presses forward*

From the middle of the century the movement took two main directions, related but each making its contribution. One of these took the form of direct action for woman suffrage and other forms of the emancipation of women. The other route was the forging ahead of some women into professions formerly occupied only by men, and their successful demonstration that the ability of women in these fields equaled that of men. These had bettter be looked at separately.

In the first category the main routes taken were public addresses, journalism, the holding of many conventions, and organization for action to get legislative changes. Throughout the larger part of the second half of the century, there were four great leaders in this field, Lucretia Mott, Elizabeth Cady Stanton, Lucy Stone, and Susan B. Anthony. They were joined by others, of lesser renown but important contributions, women like Mary A. Livermore, the Grimké sisters Angelina and Sarah, Abby Kelley Foster, and Amelia Bloomer.

Of the four principal leaders, all but Susan B. Anthony were married, and with the support of husbands who believed in their cause, each of them managed to "look well to the ways of her household" in addition to leading an active public life. I suspect that the husbands of the suffragists have probably received too little appreciation in the verdict of history for their part in the movement.

All four of these women were attractive persons, feminine in dress and appearance, and "easy on the eye" as well as engaging to the ear when they delivered the powerful addresses of which they were capable. It was before the days of the microphone but if one may judge from the hundreds who turned out to hear them, they managed their voices so that they were heard!

Mrs. Mott, older by some twenty years than the others, continued to preach with Quaker simplicity and power and to speak for her chosen causes. She was an uncompromising abolitionist, and in this capacity she traveled thousands of miles, held meetings in some of the slave states, and was sometimes in the midst of mobs and violence. She and her able but less famous husband had in their home for a time an underground railway station for escaping slaves. She continued in public life until she was well past eighty, speaking often in behalf of the woman's movement. Though less in the center of the organizational structure of the movement than the other three, she contributed much to it through her speaking but perhaps most of all through her personality.

Elizabeth Cady Stanton had seven children, and in between such withdrawals from public life as were necessary for domestic reasons, she spoke vigorously on the themes nearest her heart, temperance, the education of women, divorce, slavery, and suffrage—with the last in the ascendancy. She repeatedly addressed the New York State Legislature, which Emma Willard thirty years earlier had not been permitted to do, and was often in evidence at the numerous Women's Rights Conventions which succeeded the one she had inaugurated. A skillful writer, she contributed articles to various periodicals in addition to the *Woman's Journal,* which for many years was an important organ of the movement, and her book, *Eminent Women of the Age,* preserved much valuable information. She shocked many by espousing birth control and less rigid divorce laws long before this became respectable, and did not hesitate to challenge the Bible for being a bulwark of male supremacy.[17] Partly for such *avant-garde* attitudes, but also from differences in suffragist strategy, the movement in 1869 split into two groups, the more radical wing led by Mrs. Stanton and Miss Anthony and the other by Lucy Stone and Julia Ward Howe.

Susan B. Anthony (1820-1906) is often credited with having been the mainstay of the suffragist movement, and in an important sense this is true. Fifteen years of her early life were spent in teaching, but since she received but eight dollars a month while the men got twenty-four to thirty dollars she did not find this lucrative or satisfying.[18] Her public efforts during this period were in behalf of temperance, which remained a lifelong concern. But with the Women's Rights Convention of 1848, a new field of effort was opened to her. From 1852 on, she was the chief organizer and strategist of the women's rights movement. She served as its secretary and general agent for many years, and convened or presided over many a convention. Usually in agreement with Mrs. Stanton, she could dissent when she felt it to be necessary.[19] Less eloquent and perhaps less charismatic than the other primary leaders, she could plan political strategy, speak, interview, or organize as the occasion required. Without her untiring efforts to secure more liberal legislation, it is doubtful that the others could have accomplished what they did. History has rightly accorded her a place that is unsurpassed in the suffragist movement.

Lucy Stone Blackwell (1818-1893) is best known as Lucy Stone because she kept her maiden name and thus ushered in a practice for women in public life which has lasted to the present. At Oberlin College she became a close friend of Antoinette Brown, the first ordained woman preacher, and they married brothers,

Henry and Samuel Blackwell. Lucy's marriage was a love match with Henry sharing her views, but she kept her former name because she felt that a woman's individuality is identified with her name. For a time after her marriage she retired from public life, and their daughter Alice Stone Blackwell was to become a well-known champion of women's rights in the next generation. But before and after this period she was a flaming evangelist for the cause. Mrs. Stanton, in the book mentioned above, says of her, "She was the first speaker who really stirred the nation's heart on the subject of woman's wrongs. Young, magnetic, eloquent, her soul filled with the new idea, she drew immense audiences, and was eulogized everywhere by the press." [20] Her petite figure and dainty appearance amazed her audiences, who perhaps expected to see some sort of Amazon.

Lucy Stone was the founder and for many years one of the editors of the *Woman's Journal*. She could write as well as speak with fervor, logic, and persuasiveness. An editorial from the presidential election year of 1876 not only demonstrates her spirit but reminds us of the status of women in the years before suffrage was won. It says in part:

"Women of the United States, never forget that you are excluded by law from participation in the great question which at this moment agitates the whole country,—a question which is not only who the next candidate for president shall be, but what shall be the policy of the government for the next four years. . . .

"The interest transcends every merely personal thing. When the selection is made. and the kind of government we are to have during the next four years is indicated, every man holds his vote ready to help settle the question. He may be learned or ignorant, wise or foolish, drunken or sober: the beggar at the gate, and the thief out of jail, every man of them has his vote. But for you, every woman of you, the dog on your rug, or the cat in your corner, has as much political power as you have. Never forget it. And when the country is shaken, as it will be for months to come, over the issue, never forget that this law-making power settles every interest of yours. It settles, from the crown of your head to the sole of your feet, every personal right. It settles your relation to and right in your child. You earn or inherit a dollar; this same power decides how much of it shall be yours, and how much it will itself take or dispose of for its own use. Oh, women, the one subjugated class in this great country, the only adult people who are ruled over! pray for a baptism of fire to reveal to you the depth of the humiliation, the degradation, and the unspeakable loss which comes of your unequal position." [21]

This was in the centennial year of 1876; the antislavery issue had supposedly been won while the subjugation of women had not. This may reinforce the view that even today, the race question may be solved before that of the status of women. However, I have quoted this rather lengthy passage to remind women readers of how the matter of suffrage looked a hundred years ago, and I hope to arouse them from lethargy in the exercise of a franchise won at such cost.

In the Grimké sisters, Angelina (1805-1879) and Sarah (1805-1879),[22] we backtrack a bit in time and move into a different cultural climate. All the women presented thus far lived in the northeastern states, though they made journeys into other areas to present their causes. The Grimkés were the daughters of a Southern slave-owner who held an important judicial position in South Carolina, and were Episcopalians by inheritance. On a visit to Philadelphia Sarah became a

103

Quaker, whereupon Angelina followed her into that fold. The two became ardent abolitionists, attacking slavery from the vantage point of their Southern background. When they acquired slaves as part of the family estate in 1836, they promptly freed them and came North to lecture on the evils of slavery.

A problem soon developed. In Massachusetts, as long as they kept to the slavery issue, they were welcome, but when they began also to talk on women's rights, it was another matter. Some of the opposition came from their abolitionist friends, who feared that such talk would draw support away from the main cause. Theodore Weld, an ardent abolitionist, married Angelina, perhaps hoping to silence her on the woman question. When the sisters continued to speak and to write along both lines they incurred the disfavor of the Council of Congregational Ministers, who in a pastoral letter declared their displeasure. "The power of woman is her dependence, flowing from the consciousness of that weakness which God has given her for her protection." The Christian woman was commended "in all such associated efforts as become the modesty of her sex," but was told that when she "assumes the place and tone of a man as a public reformer, she yields her claim for protection and her character becomes unnatural." [23]

Abby Kelley Foster is one of the unsung heroines of the movement who, like the Grimké sisters, was speaking out against slavery and for women's rights before the Seneca Falls Convention. In fact, there is some evidence that she and Angelina Grimké were the first American women who dared to speak in public. For this she received not only verbal but physical missiles thrown at her in the form of eggs or decomposed fruit. After the issuance of the pastoral letter just mentioned, one overzealous clergyman preached a sermon against her with a text drawn from Revelation 2:20, "I have a few things against thee, because thou sufferest that woman, Jezebel, which calleth herself a prophetess, to teach and to seduce my servants to commit fornication." But she kept on in spite of opposition and even persecution for some fifty years. When she died in 1887, Lucy Stone at her memorial service quoted words which had been fitly spoken by Mrs. Foster herself at a Women's Rights Convention, "Sisters, bloody feet have worn smooth the path by which you come up here!" [24]

Of Mrs. Amelia Bloomer, almost everybody knows that she promoted a distinctive costume for women and thereby unintentionally introduced a word bearing her name into the English language. The outfit was devised as an emancipation from the long hooped skirt, and thus had a reasonable point. It was modest enough—full ankle-length Turkish trousers covered by a knee-length skirt. But it never became popular for it was frightfully ugly. Lucy Stone tried it but gave it up.

Not so many people know that Mrs. Bloomer was an able and enterprising editor and journalist. Her paper, *The Lily,* was the first one to be owned and operated in all its departments by a woman and served as an organ of the interests of women. Its files furnished valuable information about the woman's movement as it developed. She was also a speaker of considerable competence, and a friend and associate of Susan B. Anthony. An incident is on record of their having been denied permission to be seated, though regularly elected as delegates, at a male Temperance Convention in Syracuse in 1852, whereupon somebody generously offered them a church in which to voice their sentiments.

The result was that they drew the crowds, leaving scarcely fifty people to attend the convention.

Mrs. Mary A. Livermore, the wife of a Universalist minister, was a woman of many talents and remarkable energy. She was a powerful lecturer in behalf of abolition, temperance, and woman suffrage. She preached occasionally in her husband's pulpit and others, though she was not ordained. She was associate editor of his paper, *The New Covenant,* and for a time was editor-in-chief of the *Woman's Journal.* During the Civil War she was very active in visiting and bringing cheer to wounded men in the hospitals, and she organized ten Sanitary Fairs in various cities which raised nearly a half-million dollars to provide for their care.

Mrs. Livermore was also a leader in a movement which was becoming increasingly important. Women's clubs had begun to be formed which were concerned with the general advancement of women, not only in suffrage, but in business, professional, and social life. A Woman's Congress was called in New York in 1873, from which emerged the Association for the Advancement of Women. Mrs. Livermore was its first president, to be followed by the noted astronomer Maria Mitchell, and Julia Ward Howe. This organization lasted for twenty-six years. Its annual meetings brought together many able women, and it spawned a large number of local women's clubs and other organizations. Eventually, however, it gave way to the General Federation of Women's Clubs.

4. *Women enter the professions*

It is time now to look more closely at the entrance of women into various forms of professional life. Many women were demonstrating they could enter fields formerly closed to men, and in them do work fully equal in quality to that of men. Mrs. Hanaford in *Daughters of America* presents glimpses of the achievements of hundreds of such women in more than a score of occupations. The limits of space permit us here only a brief look at what was happening in three of the most time-honored and hence traditional of the male occupations, medicine, law, and the ministry of the churches.

Medicine was the exclusive prerogative of men up to the middle of the nineteenth century with two exceptions—large numbers of midwives who assisted in bringing into the world the large numbers of babies being born, and the dispensers of home remedies and poultices on a neighborly basis who were both cheaper and more accessible than doctors. The latter group could hardly be termed professional. As the supply of trained male physicians increased, the midwives lost prestige and their numbers diminished. At the same time there was a "felt need" for women physicians. Why? Because in a day more modest than ours, many women so disliked to consult a man on their intimate ailments or expose their bodies to the male gaze that they would go without a doctor if they could defer this necessity.

Who did it first? Dr. Elizabeth Blackwell (1821-1910) has long had this reputation, with her sister Emily a close second. What a remarkable family the Blackwells must have been! They were the sisters of Henry and Sam Blackwell, and thus the sisters-in-law of Lucy Stone and Antoinette Brown. But were they really the first woman doctors? It depends on how we reckon it.

Long before Elizabeth Blackwell, apparently from about 1835, Harriot Hunt (1805-1875) had been practicing medicine illegally because she could not induce a medical school to accept her on account of her sex. She was no novice. She had acquired a medical education by private instruction and was so successful that she built up a very lucrative practice. As a result, she had property to be taxed. Feeling keenly the injustice of "taxation without representation" because women were denied the vote, she sent in her taxes every year with a written protest to this effect, and kept it up for more than twenty-five years.

Harriot Hunt did eventually receive an M.D. degree though later than Elizabeth Blackwell. Denied admission at Harvard in 1847, she tried again in 1850 and almost succeeded. She was about to be admitted when it was discovered that a Negro man had also applied. To take such a risk on two such "never befores" was too much! Miss Hunt was asked to withdraw her application and complied. However, a Female Medical College had been started in Boston in 1848, mainly to give scientific training to midwives, and two years later one with the same name but a higher academic level was opened in Philadelphia. In 1853 the Philadelphia school conferred on her an M.D. degree.

Elizabeth Blackwell also at first studied medicine privately while teaching music and French, though she did not attempt a practice. In 1847 she applied and was refused admission at a medical school in Philadelphia, though a professor of anatomy was enough interested in her to let her practice dissection in his private laboratory. She tried other schools and was again refused. But late in 1847 her opportunity came. The dean of the medical department of a college at Geneva, N.Y., wrote her that he was submitting her request to the medical students and if none objected she might come.

The students apparently thought it was an enormous joke, and with one exception whom the rest cuffed and mauled until he changed his vote, they said they would receive her. Their unanimity may have been based on humor and curiosity, but in any case they treated her with respect when she arrived, though the townspeople did not. In 1849 she graduated at the head of her class in scholarship. She declined to walk in the academic procession lest it appear "too unladylike."

But Elizabeth Blackwell's troubles were not over. After further study in England and France, she opened a private practice in New York. Patients came slowly, and other physicians frowned upon her, whether through long tradition or fear of female rivalry. Lacking any professional companionship, she was lonely. In 1853 she opened a dispensary of her own, the New York Dispensary for Poor Women and Children. In this enterprise she was joined by her sister Emily, who had meanwhile secured a medical education in Edinburgh, and the Blackwells were off to a great career as pioneers in medicine. When the Civil War broke out, Dr. Elizabeth almost immediately enlisted the services of large numbers of women by organizing the Women's Central Association for Relief, which became an important arm of the famous Sanitary Commission. She merits all the honors history has given her.[25]

Once the barriers were down, more women became physicians. In law the movement was slower and followed a somewhat different course. Apparently not many women felt attracted to this profession, whether from sensing that they would be at a disadvantage in legal battles with men or from lack of feeling a primary need in this field. By the 1870s, when women began in any numbers to take up this profession, it was relatively easy to be admitted to law school but very difficult to be admitted to the bar.

Apparently the first woman to be graduated from a law school was Ada Kepley, from Union College in Chicago, in 1870, but I know nothing more of her. However, the year before that, Mrs. Arabella Mansfield had been admitted to the bar in Iowa, having acquired the requisite qualifications in a private office. The terms under which she was admitted should have become normative for her sex, though they did not. The Court held that the statute providing for the licensing of "any white male person" of proper qualifications could be extended to her because of another statute specifying that "words importing the masculine gender only may be extended to females." Had this statute and this interpretation become universal, the woman suffrage battle could have ended then and there, and the Equal Rights Amendment for which women have contended since 1923 would not be necessary!

By the 1870 decade the public had become fairly well accustomed to women doctors, but aspiring women lawyers still had to struggle to acquire an opportunity to employ their skills beyond clerical work in law offices. The best known of those who won the battle to secure recognition and something like equality was Belva Lockwood.

Mrs. Lockwood (1830-1917), married at eighteen to U. H. McNall and widowed at twenty-two, was a teacher and school administrator for sixteen years. During this period she did much teaching and other work in her local church along with her school duties, and during the Civil War was very active in organizing the relief activities of women. In 1868 she was married again to Dr. Ezekiel Lockwood and moved to Washington, D.C.

After the birth and death of a child, finding no consolation in this bereavement except in mental exertion, she decided to study law. She applied for admission to Columbia College but was refused on the ground that "her presence would distract the attention of the students." The next year the National University Law School was opened with provision made for admitting a few women students. There she received her law degree.

Getting admitted to the bar was another matter, but after some wangling the Supreme Court of the District of Columbia licensed her to practice. The Court of Claims in 1875 refused her application on the ground, first, that she was a woman and second, that she was a married woman with legal rights vested solely in her husband. She then began working to get a bill passed by Congress that would admit women to the bar of the United States Supreme Court. It took three years, but she succeeded and was the first recipient of this honor. Well known by this time as a lawyer, she did much to promote temperance, peace, and woman suffrage.

A considerable amount can be said of the preaching and ordination of women. The interested reader will find a longer account in my article entitled "Pioneer Women in the Ministry," mentioned earlier. We shall come to this subject again when we take up the developments of the twentieth century and the theological aspects of the status of women.

We have already had occasion to speak of the preaching of Lucretia Mott, Quaker, and Mary Livermore, Universalist. These two groups, because of their greater freedom from ecclesiastical dogma and control, seem to have produced more women preachers in the nineteenth century than any of the more conventional de-

111

nominations. The Congregational Church with its emphasis on local self-government was also open to this possibility, and this church ordained the first woman on September 15, 1853.

Antoinette Brown (1825-1921) was determined both to secure a college education and to become a minister. Oberlin College provided the opportunity to satisfy the first of these ambitions. But what of the second? After much protest from the "Ladies' Board" as well as the faculty, she was permitted to take theological courses but not with credit toward a degree. After an interval of social work, lecturing on social causes, and occasionally preaching, she was invited to serve a small Congregational church at South Butler, N.Y., at a salary of $300 a year. There she was duly ordained, with considerable publicity for which Horace Greeley sent reporters from the *New York Tribune.*

She soon had warm friends in the parish who accepted her. But trouble arose, partly from her sex but also from her theology which did not accord with the dour Calvinism that was prevalent. She resigned her parish, returned to her former work in the slums and to lecturing, and was courted by Samuel Blackwell. To summarize her subsequent career, she married Sam; bore six children; resumed preaching, this time in a Unitarian church; wrote nine books, two of them in scientific fields; received a belated B.D. degree from Oberlin in 1908; preached her last sermon at ninety; and died at ninety-six after having lived long enough to see the Woman Suffrage Amendment passed for which she had so often spoken.

Another pioneer woman preacher was Olympia Brown (1835-1926), a younger contemporary of Antoinette and a Universalist. Educated at Mount Holyoke

Seminary and Antioch College, she was admitted with some reluctance to the theological school of St. Lawrence University at Canton, N.Y., and was ordained there upon her graduation in 1863. She is credited with unusual intellectual acumen. She held several pastorates, married John H. Willis though she kept her maiden name, and demonstrated that it was quite possible to combine a successful pastorate with marriage and motherhood. Her Alma Mater did her belated honor by celebrating the centennial of her ordination with considerable publicity, a bronze plaque, and a scholarship established in her name.

Mrs. Phebe A. Hanaford, to whose book on women of the century this chapter is much indebted, was also an outstanding Universalist minister, with an amazing list of "firsts" among her achievements. Besides serving three pastorates for considerable periods, she was the author of a dozen books, a leader in her denomination, and for a time the regularly appointed chaplain of the Connecticut Legislature. She tells us of having officiated at the funeral of the oldest Free Mason in America, and from a later source comes a touch that shows how these pioneer women were bound together. At the funeral of Elizabeth Cady Stanton in 1902, the Rev. Antoinette Brown Blackwell spoke, and at the grave, the Rev. Phebe A. Hanaford.

We can only mention other women preachers of that day. There was the Quaker Sybil Jones, aunt of Rufus M. Jones. She traveled widely with his uncle Eli, and some found her easier to listen to than her husband. There was "the silver-tongued Sarah Smiley," also a Quaker though she consented to be baptized, in whom good looks, brains, and a determined Christian purpose apparently converged. There was Anna Snowden, better known as Anna Oliver, who took this name not by marriage but by choice to avoid embarrassing her parents when she decided to study theology and become a preacher. She was a Methodist, as was also Maggie Van Cott, of whom we learn that she did a phenomenal amount of evangelistic preaching, traveling, and holding of meetings. These women were no weaklings!

Yet with all these achievements, there was as yet little ordination of women, no woman suffrage, only meager recognition of the quality of women in the professions or other public relationships. Was it to be better in the next century, as they all seem to have expected? We shall see.

V Advance and retreat

In the previous chapter we have traced the rise of women to opportunities long denied them, and have given some snapshots of remarkable women of the nineteenth century who took the lead in these advances. It was a truly great century. But what of the twentieth?

We find some important changes as we come closer to our own times. The woman suffrage movement after a long struggle came to fruition in the adoption of the Susan B. Anthony Amendment—better known as the Nineteenth—in 1920. Then the women's rights movement simmered down, and little more was heard of it until the 1960s. The women of today, having now had the vote for fifty years, are apt simply to take it for granted as if women had always voted.

Meanwhile, the movement of women into many forms of business and professional life expanded enormously. College education became almost as much the order of the day for girls as for boys, whether in women's colleges or coeducational schools. Few professional schools of any kind debarred women because of their sex, though in most they remained a small minority. As a result, there were few forms of occupation except those requiring masculine muscular strength in which women were not to be found. This did not mean equality in status, pay, promotion, or opportunities for creative leadership—hence the Women's Liberation Movement of the present. Nevertheless, the rigid barriers of an earlier day went down.

In the churches, there were great advances in the form of the women's voluntary organizations, functioning mainly through lay women in the local congregations. There were both advances and retreats in the matter of the ordination and ministry of women. Women won representation in church assemblies, but their number remained small—often no more than a token representation. All these movements are today in flux.

In this chapter we shall look at the first and third of these major developments. The movement of women into many forms of occupation outside the home is both too broad to permit any brief summary and too familiar to require it. But the woman suffrage movement should not be left in midstream, and the place of women in the churches is a central motif of our study.

1. *Woman suffrage is won*

As indicated in the previous chapter, the woman's movement in 1869 split into two groups, one led by Mrs. Stanton and Miss Anthony, the other by Lucy Stone and Julia Ward Howe.[1] They remained personal friends but differed in strategy. The Stanton-Anthony organization was called the National Woman Suffrage Association, the other the American Woman Suffrage Association. In 1890 they merged again to form the National American Woman Suffrage Association (hereafter referred to as NAWSA), and this lasted until the main objective was won in 1920.

But why the split? It was due partly to a difference between radical and more conservative elements in the movement—a tendency which seems perennially to divide groups with a common objective. But it was due also to a factor that was to pursue the movement for years to come and is still visible—the interplay between the woman's movement and the racial demand for equality and justice.[2]

After the Civil War, when the Fourteenth Amendment to give the Negro citizenship rights was drafted, the word "male" was inserted. The suffrage leaders saw that this would make the women's struggle much harder. Supporters of the Fourteenth added the Fifteenth to make it stronger, "The right of citizens . . . to vote shall not be abridged . . . on account of race, color, or previous condition of servitude." The suffragists fought valiantly to get the word "male" dropped from the first and the word "sex" inserted in the second. But they lost, and for the first time the word "male" became embedded in the Constitution. Though they worked together in an American Equal Rights Association, they differed in that Mrs. Stanton and Miss Anthony opposed the Fourteenth Amendment in that form, while Lucy Stone believed that the Negro should get his rights even if women could not.

Furthermore, they lost valuable male support over this issue. Some of their stanchist former supporters, such as Wendell Phillips and Theodore Tilton, counseled them to lay off their main objective for a time to concentrate on the Negro, and "this is the Negro's hour" began to be a phrase much bandied about. Horace Greeley withdrew his support in a personal tilt with Mrs. Stanton. From this time on, the Northern women who had supported abolition so fervently before found themselves torn emotionally and strategically, desiring to see the Negro advance toward justice but reluctant to see this happen at the cost of justice to women.

The problem became still more complicated as differences of opinion arose over the best way to secure woman suffrage. Was it to be by the gradual process of state by state action, or by a federal amendment to the Constitution? Obviously this was a case of an issue that persists to the present—states rights versus federal government—as well as of the most effective strategy. The Northern women were divided on the question. But as more and more Southern women became members of NAWSA and could influence its policy, they insisted on the state by state position. Committed to white supremacy by culture and long tradition, some wanted the word "white" inserted in any franchise a state might grant, but when the Fifteenth Amendment forestalled that, most were willing to see the Negro vote limited by educational and literacy requirements. A political argument often used was that since there were more white women in the South than Negro men and women combined, extending the franchise to women would increase the white majority in the electorate.[3]

Meanwhile, other important developments were taking place. Woman suffrage constitutional amendments were adopted by a number of states, mainly in the West, and in the East and Midwest potent new forces of opposition were rising to power. Also, some strong new leaders were emerging as the original pioneers of the woman's movement were being removed by old age or death.

Wyoming adopted woman suffrage as a territory in 1869 and carried it into statehood in 1890, thus becoming the first state to extend the electorate to women. Colorado adopted it by constitutional amendment in 1893 and Idaho in 1896, and Utah on achieving statehood in 1896. For fourteen years these were the only states where women could vote, but after various defeats there came quite a spurt in this direction—Washington in 1910, California in 1911, Oregon, Kansas, and Arizona in 1912, Montana and Nevada in 1914.

Such action by the Western states, mainly by amendments to their constitutions, indicates the degree to which the suffrage idea had taken hold. It did not happen automatically, for "the women conducted many state campaigns, securing signatures on petitions, traveling over the immense western distances in bad weather and with dreadful transportation, speaking again and again before voters and legislators." [4] Usually they were defeated. Yet little by little, the movement advanced.

But why in the West rather than the East and North which had been the seedbed of the movement? Doubtless the less tradition-bound climate of the newer states was a major factor. But other sociological factors reflect new forces to be contended with.

One of these was the rising power of the liquor interests. However much strong drink was consumed in the West, the center of its vested interests was in the East and Midwest. As an indirect compliment to the power of the votes of women, these interests fought the suffrage movement at every step. Likewise for many a temperance advocate, "Wait till the women vote!" was a cry of hope and expectation. As the Prohibition movement arose, many able women were identified with both causes, and it is no accident that the Eighteenth and Nineteenth Amendments were finally passed in the same year.[5]

Foremost among such women was Frances E. Willard (1839-1898). An officer of the Woman's Christian Temperance Union from its founding in 1874, she was its President from 1879 until her death and built it into

119

an organization that had much respect and influence. Before this became her principal activity she was an outstanding educator at Northwestern University, and in 1905 her statue was placed in the rotunda of the Capitol at Washington to represent the state of Illinois.

A further factor in the changing social climate of the East and Midwest was the influx of large numbers of foreign-born immigrants, predominantly from southern and eastern Europe and different in language, religion, and culture. But the suffrage movement, like the temperance and before it the abolitionist, was largely the effort of white Anglo-Saxon Protestants, though no one had as yet begun to speak of WASPs. The new immigrants from their European background were predisposed to favor neither woman suffrage nor temperance, and voted against both. Furthermore, they often became easy plunder for the manipulation of the liquor interests and the party machines.

This created a fresh battleground for the suffrage movement. Analysis of election returns by precincts showed clearly that foreign-born voters were using their franchise to defeat the woman's movement. The natural result was indignation and dismay. The argument could be used that cultured and well-educated women, descendants of the early colonists and of Revolutionary heroes, were being denied the vote while ignorant male voters of no American heritage had it. Another argument began to appear, a close replica to what Southern suffragists had used against the Negro—that women must have the vote to keep a preponderance of native-born Americans in the electorate, and educational and literacy tests must be imposed. Not all looked at it this way. Jane Addams of Hull House in Chicago campaigned for suffrage on the ground that foreign-born women as

120

well as others must have the vote to clean up the slums and make America a country in which all could live in greater health, dignity, and opportunity.[6]

A situation so complex required strong leadership. This was forthcoming. As in the earlier stages, many more women contributed to the movement than can be mentioned here. But in addition to Frances Willard and Jane Addams whose primary work was elsewhere, there were again four suffrage leaders of outstanding ability, determination, and influence.

Dr. Anna Howard Shaw (1847-1919) forms a bridge between the old regime and the new. Growing up on the Michigan frontier, she early decided she wanted to be a minister. With great hardship she worked her way through Albion College and Boston University School of Theology. Though not permitted ordination in her denomination, the Methodist Episcopal, she was ordained in the Methodist Protestant Church in 1880. She held two pastorates in Massachusetts, but being impressed with the sickness she saw in the slums of Boston, she decided to study medicine and earned an M.D. degree, also at Boston University. Still feeling keenly the need of large-scale social changes for which she believed the votes of women were needed, she then gave the remainder of her life to the suffrage movement. She was an orator of unusual power, logical, witty, of commanding persuasiveness as she addressed hundreds of audiences across the nation. But she was also drafted for administrative duties. She was President of NAWSA during the years 1904 to 1915, and in this period seven states took action for woman suffrage. Hoping for less arduous responsibilities, she gave up her office in 1915, but as soon as America entered the war, President Wilson drafted her as chairman of the Women's Committee of the National Council of Defense. She threw herself into this with the same zeal as before, but died soon after the war ended.

Mention was made in the previous chapter of the establishment of the *Woman's Journal* by Lucy Stone. Founded in 1870, it had as its first editor-in-chief Mrs. Mary Livermore, but when she could no longer carry it, it reverted to Lucy Stone and her husband Henry Blackwell. They managed it until their daughter Alice Stone Blackwell could take it over. She was its editor through the crucial years we are now considering.

Alice Stone Blackwell (1857-1950) is less well known than her mother. But she rendered a service of incalculable value in the *Journal,* especially through her editorials, which were sane, balanced, and vigorous without being vicious. At a time when cross currents could have split the movement wide open and wrecked it, she helped to hold it together on a seaworthy keel. Another unusual talent gave her an important responsibility—to answer questions from the floor after a public address. She could respond quickly and appropriately, and thus turned many an attack into something favorable to the cause.[7]

Carrie Chapman Catt (1859-1947) was the generalissima who brought the suffrage movement through to victory. She began her public career by teaching and becoming Superintendent of Schools in Mason City, Iowa —an unusual post for a woman, whether then or now, and an evidence of her remarkable administrative skill. Her first husband, Leo Chapman, died soon after their marriage and her second husband, George Catt, believed in the suffrage cause enough to be willing to have her give considerable time to it.

Since the reunion of the two divisions of the movement and the formation of NAWSA in 1890, at first Mrs. Stanton and then Susan B. Anthony had been its President. By 1900 she was eighty years old and ready to turn the responsibility over to other hands. She retired with a tremendous outpouring of appreciation for her services of almost fifty years, and Mrs. Catt was elected in her place. Her tenure at that time was brief, for both her own health and the illness of her husband caused her to resign in 1904. He died the next year, but Dr. Shaw had succeeded her as President, and Mrs. Catt for a decade gave her services of leadership primarily to the international suffrage movement. When Dr. Shaw laid down the gavel in 1915, Mrs. Catt was the obvious choice to replace her, and she led the movement to its fruition in 1920. During the rest of her long life she worked actively for peace.

Mrs. Catt was a person of such gentility and restraint that she won the respect of conservatives who did not agree with her views. But she was also a person of great determination and courage, and of remarkable political finesse. We cannot trace here all the steps by which she won the eventual support of President Wilson, who believed in the suffragist movement with his mind but not his emotions. By a bipartisan approach she won backing from both sides. The male politicians of the 1970s might well take some lessons from her!

But it was not all smooth sailing, and there were differences of policy within the movement. While Dr. Shaw was still the President of NAWSA, a Congressional Union had been formed, which later broke with NAWSA to form the National Woman's Party. Alice Paul, a much younger woman, was its guiding spirit.

We must go back a little to get the setting. For years a federal amendment later bearing the name of Susan B.

Anthony had been kept before Congress but without success.[8] It was straightforward and clear. It read:

Section 1. The right of citizens of the United States to vote shall not be denied or abridged by the United States or by any State on account of sex.

Section 2. Congress shall have power to enforce this article by appropriate legislation.

Year after year, the Judiciary Committee of the House of Representatives rejected or pigeonholed it. Meanwhile, most of the energy of NAWSA went into the passage of state constitutional amendments which had a better chance to win.

Alice Paul and the National Woman's Party would have no such temporizing. They insisted that there must be an all-out effort for a federal amendment. Mrs. Catt and NAWSA agreed with this objective but were skeptical of the methods of the National Woman's Party.

Alice Paul was a Quaker with a B.A. from Swarthmore and a Ph.D. from the University of Pennsylvania, and a dedicated activist. Between these degrees she studied in England, and while there she engaged in militant activity with the British suffragettes. She served three prison terms, went on a hunger strike and was forcibly fed. She returned to America firmly resolved to secure the passage of a federal suffrage amendment.

Miss Paul's strategy was to enlist the votes of the women in the enfranchised states as a threat to the dominant party, to send delegations and then to picket the White House until President Wilson would support suffrage, and to stage massive demonstrations. The first of these strategies failed to defeat the Democrats, but the other two gave wide publicity to the movement and caused mixed reactions. The White House was picketed non-violently for many months, whereupon Miss Paul and some of her associates were thrown in jail and savagely treated.[9] On the day before President Wilson was inaugurated on March 3, 1913, early in her campaign, eight thousand women marched down Pennsylvania Avenue with the pageantry which she knew how to use effectively. The parade encountered ridicule and violence as well as applause from spectators. It is said that when President Wilson drove through empty streets to his hotel he asked, "Where are the people?" and received the answer, "Over on the Avenue watching the suffrage parade."[10]

Eventually the victory was won. The Amendment was passed by Congress on June 4, 1919 and ratified by the thirty-sixth state, Tennessee, in a dramatically close vote on August 26, 1920. But who won it—Mrs. Catt and NAWSA or Alice Paul and the National Woman's Party? It is impossible to give all the credit to either side. Each approach needed the other, and without both the long struggle might have been even longer.

What then? After 1920 NAWSA disbanded because it was no longer needed. But in 1919, on the fiftieth anniversary of the first voting by women in Wyoming, Mrs. Catt had proposed a national League of Women Voters with a nonpartisan approach to political issues. This still functions effectively on this basis. The National Woman's Party continues to the present. It has attempted since 1923 to get through Congress an Equal Rights Amendment to apply to other matters than the vote, without success until in 1970 it passed the House by a large majority, only to be bogged down in the Senate.

Yet with the passage of the Nineteenth Amendment,

the steam went out of the woman's movement. Despite many advances in professional and business life and the formation of many Women's Clubs, as a large-scale concerted effort it was dead. In a vast proliferation of other activities, most women forgot the long struggle of their earlier sisters, and while they often chafed at injustices, they did little about them until a new mood emerged in the 1960s.

2. _____ in the ministry of the church

In the famous Seneca Falls Declaration of Sentiments, the twelfth resolution, introduced and doubtless written by Mrs. Lucretia Mott, reads as follows:

Resolved, That the speedy success of our cause depends upon the zealous and untiring efforts of both men and women, for the overthrow of the monopoly of the pulpit, and for the securing to woman an equal participation with men in the various trades, professions and commerce.[11]

This was passed unanimously. Gradually women began to participate with men, even though not equally, in the various trades, professions, and commerce. But what about "the overthrow of the monopoly of the pulpit"?

As has been indicated, it was by no means unusual in the second half of the nineteenth century for women to occupy pulpits. There was resistance, but many outstanding women overcame it. We have noted that two of the most distinguished and effective leaders of the woman's movement, Lucretia Mott and Anna Howard Shaw, were ministers. Mary Livermore and Julia Ward Howe, in addition to being writers, editors, lecturers, and suf-

126

fragists of distinction, were occasional preachers, in the Universalist and Unitarian churches respectively. In 1873 Mrs. Howe brought together a group of women ministers around Boston, and this led to eight annual conventions and the formation in 1882 of the Women's Ministerial Conference. Antoinette Brown Blackwell and Phebe Hanaford, in addition to a long and effective preaching ministry, each wrote a considerable shelfful of books. Other women ministers of ability and courage were noted in the previous chapter.

This roster of able women ministers in the nineteenth century could be greatly extended. Mrs. Hanaford in *Daughters of America* mentions sixty of them by name and tells something of the life story of most of them. But with what I trust will be due restraint, I shall speak only of a few more.

Amanda Way, born in 1829, appears to have been the first woman to be given a license to preach in the Methodist Eposcopal Church—not ordination, for the General Conference was not yet ready for that. Besides preaching she held one office after another in the Good Templars—a secret temperance order—until she became the first woman to hold the highest office in the National Lodge. An early issue of the *Woman's Journal* says this of the range of her services, "The stanch advocate of progress, the friend of the slave, the champion of women's rights, priestess of temperance, indefatigable worker for the Sanitary Commission, and tireless nurse in the hospital, and on the field. It was good to look into her face, and to listen to the tones of her deep rich voice. . . ." [12] All this in addition to her preaching and pastoral ministry in Indiana and Kansas! Asked why she had never married, she replied as did Susan B. Anthony on another occasion, "I have never had time."

Lorenza Haynes, Universalist, taught school for many years and served for six years as librarian in her hometown of Waltham, Mass. In 1874, when she was fifty-four years old, she entered Canton Theological School, the only woman in her class, and graduated at its head. She served two, perhaps three, parishes and retired at seventy, but after a year of leisure a delegation of men from two adjacent former parishes entreated her to come back at any salary within reason.

Ada C. Bowles, successful pastor of the Universalist church in Easton, Pa., wrote a book on *Women in the Ministry*. However, I mention her chiefly as the prototype of a present situation. At twenty-two, in 1858, she was married to the Rev. Benjamin F. Bowles and studied theology along with him. After eleven years she began to preach, and at the height of their pastorates solved a practical marital problem by living in Philadelphia, where he had a flourishing church, and commuting to Easton.

Caroline Crane seems to have been the most modern of them all. In 1889 she went as a Unitarian minister to Kalamazoo, Mich. When her congregation had grown to the point where it could build a new church, she added to it a kindergarten, a women's gymnasium, and departments in manual training and domestic science. Later she transformed its basement into a dining room for women workers. Turning her attention beyond the church to the city, she was instrumental in getting its streets cleaned, employment found for the destitute, and greater sanitation established through meat inspection. She acquired such a reputation in these areas that she surrendered her pulpit to give full time to municipal housecleaning.

Along with such women as these, there were hundreds

of others who were doing unheralded but faithful work in the churches and communities. I shall mention but one of these, who might now be nameless except for her great influence at a strategic point. The Rev. Marianna Thompson was the minister in the small community of Big Rapids, Michigan, which was Anna Howard Shaw's hometown as a child. She inspired the young Anna not only with the thought of becoming a minister but with the ambition to get an education to prepare for this calling. What a service to the world!

Most of these women ministers of an earlier day have not left their names graven in history. Yet they did something more important—they served their churches and their generation with fidelity at the call of God. We have no way of knowing just how many of them there were, but Alice Stone Blackwell in her *Lucy Stone,* speaking of her pioneer aunt Antoinette Brown Blackwell, says, "When she died, the census showed that there were more than three thousand women ministers and preachers in the United States." [13] Mrs. Blackwell died in 1921, and this along with the suffrage victory the previous year marks a turning point between the old order and the new.

Contrary to the glowing expectations of their predecessors, the opportunities for women ministers did not increase in the twentieth century but in its early decades began to decline. In numbers the movement seems to have held fairly steady for a time, for the census statistics of 1930 reported 3,276 women clergymen, 0.2 percent of the women in all professional and near-professional occupations, and 2.2 percent of all those employed as clergy.[14] But by this time there had been a proliferation of many small sects, and in these, women were much more likely to be found as clergy than in the mainline churches.

In 1919 a nucleus of the latter group, at the initiative of the Rev. Madeline Southard who was a Methodist minister in Kansas, formed the American Association of Women Ministers. Small in numbers but rich in dedication, this organization has lasted to the present, celebrating its golden jubilee in 1969 and changing its name in 1970 to the International Association of Women Ministers. It has provided fellowship for its members, and its annual reports on "The Ecclesiastical Status of Women" prepared by its Director of Research, Dr. Hazel Foster, contain valuable history of the movement as a whole. But it has not been able to stem the movement away from the ministry as a vocation for women which has only recently reversed its direction.

Though no exact statistics are available, there are probably fewer women serving parishes today than there were at the turn of the century, though the number with some theological education is larger because for many years the major Protestant seminaries have admitted women without protest. But to have a theological degree does not ensure that one will preach, or be ordained, or even enter a religious vocation as a profession.

A current sampling will indicate the trend. In preparation of her excellent book published in 1970, *When the Minister Is a Woman,* Mrs. Elsie Gibson secured data from 270 ordained American women of various denominations. This number does not include all there are in the United States, but those to whom she could secure access by questionnaire, correspondence, or interview. Where the woman combines two functions, such as teaching and occasionally preaching, she is listed with

130

the major one. The following is the tally for those with
five or more respondents: [15]

Pastors	81
Retired	40
Ministers' wives	20
Ministers of Christian Education	18
In denominational work	16
Assistant pastors	16
Associate pastors	15
Chaplains in institutions	10
Other specialized ministries	9
Teachers in college	8
Graduate students	6
Teachers in seminary	5

The remainder are in a variety of categories—directors of Christian education, evangelists, mission work,
counseling, editors, and writers.

This list illustrates two important features of the current situation: (1) the scarcity of women in pastorates,
even among the churches that now ordain women, and
(2) the proliferation of trained women into numerous
other forms of religious work.

There are a number of reasons for this change from
earlier days. Since about 1920, to be a Director of Christian Education has been the field above all others which
a woman wishing to pursue a religious vocation in the
Protestant churches has been encouraged to enter. Many
have attended a theological seminary to secure the
needed preparation and have found employment in this
field. But many have left it again, partly from a sense
of frustration, partly from the insecurity involved. When
the church budget shrinks, the Director of Christian

Education is often the first staff member to be eliminated, and when it expands, she is apt to be replaced by an associate pastor who is a man.

Doubtless the current secularization of society has had its effect on both the preaching ministry and the Christian education services of women. As both the moral and financial support given to the churches becomes more difficult to sustain, women hesitate to enter a field which is at best precarious, and those who wish to serve from a Christian motivation are likely to take up some form of social work. Formerly much of this service was rendered by deaconesses under church auspices; now it is more likely to be under a municipal agency, distinct from any religious organization and better paid.

An obstacle to women in the ministry has arisen from an unexpected source, the ecumenical movement. This first came to my attention as long ago as the Madras International Missionary Conference of 1938. The late Dr. Hilda Ives, an exceptionally able woman minister and theological professor in rural sociology at Andover-Newton Seminary, asked to have something inserted in one of the reports giving encouragement to women in the ministry. Upon hearing her presentation the Bishop of Winchester strode to the rostrum and asked to have this defeated because such a move would cause barriers to the ecumenical movement and in particular to church union. It was defeated. Repeatedly since that time I have heard this argument used. It seems not to occur to those who use it that the argument can be reversed—if the ministry of women is supported by the ecumenical movement, more churches will embrace it and thus the total ministry of the churches will be enlarged.[16]

3. *Signs of promise*

However, I do not wish to end this chapter on a pessimistic note. There are "straws in the wind" which indicate advance in the ministry of women. And in the matter of the voluntary services of women in the local churches, there have been great advances through the decades and significant new movements in our own time.

The arguments against the ordination and ministry of women have usually been of three types: theological (the Bible, Christian doctrine, and ecclesiastical tradition forbid it) ; biological (it would not work because a woman's church and family obligations would conflict) ; and social (neither men nor women want a woman preacher). The theological objections, to be discussed more fully in a later chapter, are breaking down in the more flexible theological climate of the present. They are viewed even by some Roman Catholics as being invalid. The biological objections are no more serious here than in many other fields where women unite a professional career with childbearing and domesticity. Women have demonstrated repeatedly that it is not an insuperable barrier. The social objections remain as the chief obstacle to the appointment of women to parish pastorates, though a less serious barrier to their ordination.

As a result some important changes have taken place in recent years. In 1956 The Methodist Church, which had long ordained women as local deacons and elders and appointed them as approved supplies to serve small churches but without Annual Conference membership, suddenly removed all restrictions based on sex. With the granting of full clergy rights two unusually able Methodist women, Gusta Robinette in Sumatra and

Margaret Henrichsen in Maine,[17] became District Superintendents exercising jurisdiction over a considerable number of male ministers—and the heavens did not fall! Other dire effects which had been predicted seem not to have ensued. In the same year and almost simultaneously, the United Presbyterian Church U.S.A. (Northern) gave full ordination to women. This was the more surprising because of its greater theological rigor. Its forebear John Calvin had refused to permit women to speak in meeting, to say nothing of exercising any priestly office, and had said of what he regarded as Catholic corruptions in this matter, "It is the height of impudence to urge here the approval of earlier times, for it is plainly evident that this abuse did not become implanted except with the barbarous confusion of the whole of Christianity." [18]

Yet in 1964 the Southern Presbyterian Church followed the example of its northern neighbor. The Lutheran line had appeared fixed in its tradition, but this began to be broken by stages in the Scandinavian countries between 1958 and 1964. In 1970, both the Lutheran Church in America and the American Lutheran Church voted to ordain women. The Disciples have had official equality for women since the founding of this denomination, or brotherhood, in the early 1800s. The Congregationalists and Baptists have long ordained women, though fewer Baptist than Congregational women have availed themselves of this opportunity. The Protestant Episcopal Church is more rigid in its male tradition, though in 1970 women for the first time were permitted to sit in its House of Deputies. Counting in the Quakers, the Universalists and Unitarians now merged in one denomination, the Salvation Army, and numerous small denominations, there are now about eighty Protestant groups in America that have given official sanction to women in the ministry.

On the world scene there are many others. We cannot here go into this matter, but a summary of this roster may be found in Elsie Culver's *Women in the World of Religion*.[19] The Anglican, Eastern Orthodox, and Roman Catholic communions remain adamant, though Pope John XXIII came almost to breaching the barrier when he wrote in the encyclical *Pacem in Terris:*

Human beings have the right to choose freely the state of life which they prefer, and therefore the right to set up a family, with equal rights and duties for man and woman, and also the right to follow a vocation to the priesthood or the religious life.[20]

Had his life been spared a little longer, who knows but that by now there might be women priests, as there are now competent women theologians, in the Catholic Church.

Another important field which can only be mentioned is the extensive service rendered by Roman Catholic nuns and Lutheran and Episcopalian sisterhoods in various orders. Not only is most of the teaching in parochial schools done by these dedicated women, but much social service as well. With the lessening of restrictions as to the habits to be worn have come other adjustments to the times, though in some cases not enough to permit a happy adjustment to tradition, and hence the breaking of such ties for a freer life in service to society.

In the American Protestant churches, it is in the women's voluntary organizations for lay service in the local churches that the most spectacular and the most acceptable contributions are to be found. A Woman's Board of Foreign Missions was established among the Congregationalists in 1868; the Methodist Episcopal Women's Foreign Missionary Society came into being in 1869; a corresponding group among the northern Presbyterians in 1870; and one in the Protestant Episcopal group in 1871.[21] Similar Home Missions groups were soon established in these and most of the other Protestant churches. An ecumenical Council of Women for Home Missions was organized in 1908 and a Federation of Women's Boards of Foreign Missions of North America in 1912, thus antedating most of the ecumenical stirrings of this century. They changed their forms as the decades passed, becoming the United Church Women in 1941 and more recently Church Women United—to stress the "united for action" vigor of the movement. In thousands of communities today, women work ecumenically through this organization, particularly in the observance of three special days—the World Day of Prayer the first Friday in March, the May Fellowship the first Friday in May, and World Community Day the first Friday in November.

The traditional early division in local churches into home and foreign missionary societies and "Ladies Aid" for local service has in most cases given way to a comprehensive women's fellowship, variously called by such names as the Women's Society of Christian Service or the Women's Association. Here is a very vigorous arm of Christian outreach, usually with a national board and regional officers that hold conferences at various levels and promote study and action in the local churches. When compared with the men's clubs to be found in some local churches, most observers would say that the strength of these women's associations is beyond comparison.

One could go further and point out that, in spite of this eminent service of women in and to the churches, their representation in both ecumenical and denominational governing bodies is very small. The statistics are available—but why bother to give them? One has only to attend one of these gatherings and look around to discover the disparity, both in lay representation as compared with that of the clergy and, where the numerical equality of laity and clergy is fixed by governing rules, in the small proportion of lay women delegates to lay men.

Instead of laboring this point, I prefer to end this chapter, and with it the historical division of the book, on a more optimistic note. Let us for a moment recall Mary Wollstonecraft's word of 1792, "Men, in general, seem to employ their reason to justify prejudices, which they have imbibed, they cannot trace how, rather than root them out." And let us reflect that many men of today both in the churches and in society—I could name hundreds of them if it were appropriate—have not only recognized their prejudices but have used their voices and their votes for the fuller equality of women. Let us be grateful to them. There will have to be more such men before all the prejudices will give way to justice— *there will be more of them!*

VI The Bible and the status of women

We have now traced in outline the history of the social status of women from the earliest times to the present. Even so brief a survey must have made evident how deeply embedded the subordination of women is in our cultural inheritance. On the one hand, this explains why this subordination is so widely held to, with the assumption that "woman's place is the home," and only there. On the other, what has happened in the past hundred and fifty years is the record of a determined, long-range effort by many women and their male supporters to secure greater justice grounded in the equality of persons.

This narration of events has made it necessary to look at the Bible from the standpoint of practices and attitudes reflected in both the Old and New Testaments. But we must now approach the matter from another angle.

From the standpoint of Christian faith, it is essential to consider not only what has happened in the past but what ought to happen if the insights and norms inherent in this faith are to be taken seriously. For this reason, this division of the book aims to approach the matter of the status of women in church and society from a theological viewpoint.

The Bible is not the only foundation of Christian faith. This faith is grounded in the totality of God's world and the living stream of human experience. It is supremely grounded in the revelation of God in Jesus Christ, "in whose light we see light." Yet it is the Bible that gives us the record of "the Christ event," and the Bible as variously interpreted has gone far toward shaping both popular thought and Christian theology through the past two millennia of history. It is appropriate, therefore, that we begin a theological inquiry at this point.

1. *The stance for biblical interpretation*

We have noted how frequently the Bible, and in particular the words of Paul, have been quoted in opposition to the public activity of women, including the right to vote. The suffrage battle was won fifty years ago, but in the churches women are still largely denied places of leadership in pulpits and church councils and assemblies. Biblical literalism is less prevalent than formerly, but it is not dead. Its effects survive in ecclesiastical practices and attitudes so deeply embedded that their eradication may require an even longer struggle than that by which the franchise was won.

A bit of further history may serve as an introduction to biblical and theological consideration of the status of women. In the later years of the nineteenth century, the historical approach to the Bible, generally known as higher criticism, was beginning to be in vogue among theologians and biblical scholars.[1] This was viewed as heretical among those whom we now call fundamentalists, and ordinary Christians when they heard of it were inclined to view it askance as something criticizing the Bible. But the leaders of the suffrage movement saw in it a chance to answer the Bible-quoting anti-suffragists! They could take one of three courses, or any combination of the three. They could say (1) that there had been incorrect translations, or (2) that certain statements in the Bible were the product of historical circumstances instead of being the infallible Word of God, or (3) that Paul, being a man and therefore fallible like other men, was mistaken in his estimate of women.

These defenders of woman suffrage, though they were not weighty biblical scholars, were not wrong in their contentions. Yet in their zeal to answer anti-suffrage critics who were quoting the Bible to support their opposition, some of its defenders adopted a procedure which made foes instead of friends for the suffrage movement.

Elizabeth Cady Stanton, born in 1815, was well along in years in the 1890s, but with her accustomed vigor she seized upon this channel for answering the critics and defending the cause to which she had given a lifetime of effort. She was not an atheist, and she had much sympathy with the position of her friend Lucretia Mott who had said that she preferred "resting on truth as authority, rather than taking authority for truth." [2] But she was more secular in her approach than most of the other leaders, and she felt resentment that both the Bible and the church had erected barriers to human justice in the matter of the equality of women, as had earlier been the case in regard to slavery.

Lucretia Mott was gone by this time, and Susan B. Anthony tried to dissuade Mrs. Stanton from a course that she believed inappropriate. But to no avail. Mrs. Stanton proposed the issuance of a *Woman's Bible* and she secured the cooperation of a Revising Committee to prepare it. The word "revising" was intended to be taken in its etymological meaning of "reviewing" or "viewing again," and the *Woman's Bible* was not a rewritten

140

Bible but an extensive commentary on those portions dealing with women. Part I covering the Pentateuch was issued in 1895. It was the responsibility of a Revising Committee of twenty-three women, though probably not more than eight actually wrote it. The list contains such familiar names as Mrs. Stanton herself, the Rev. Phebe Hanaford, the Rev. Olympia Brown, Mary A. Livermore, Carrie Chapman Catt, and another woman preacher, the Rev. Augusta Chapin, in addition to the two previously mentioned.

The result was predictable. Many people were shocked at such heresy, and the woman's movement lost rather than gained friends. When Part II covering the rest of the Bible appeared in 1898, several names of the original committee including those of Mrs. Livermore and Mrs. Catt were absent from the list. Meanwhile in 1896 NAWSA had adopted a resolution declaring that the Association, being wholly nonsectarian, "has no official connection with the so-called 'Woman's Bible' or any theological publication." Miss Anthony showed her loyalty to her friend by opposing the resolution as an unnecessary repudiation of a privately published work and an affront to the honorary president of the Association, but it passed.[3]

After this digression, let us "review" what the Bible says about women and the equality or inequality of the sexes.

Both textual and historical studies have now advanced so far beyond what they were in the nineteenth century that one may appeal to them without apology, and, indeed, under necessity if one is to give anything like a true appraisal of the relevant biblical passages. Recent translations, particularly the Revised Standard Version and the remarkable New English Bible, can be trusted to give a more accurate construing of texts than was formerly available. That the Bible as a whole shows marks of the social setting in which it was produced over a period of more than a thousand years and by many authors is now agreed upon by those who make a serious study of it. This is not to deny its deep and permanent insights, but it precludes any superficial view of its verbal inspiration and literal infallibility. As this historical approach to the Bible has gained acceptance, it has answered many questions and afforded a deeper appreciation of its revelatory character as a disclosure of the nature and reality of God, at work within the human scene.

In particular, this approach has thrown fresh light on the meaning and importance of myth in the Bible. Myth does not mean simply legend, or a relic of primitive superstition. Myth means the disclosure of truth in pictorial, poetic, and often highly artistic form, but it is not literal history or objective scientific information. To take it with these connotations is to distort its true meaning. A literary myth usually comes out of the experience of a people without specific authorship, and reflects convictions long held and transmitted through story rather than history. Such is the case with the mythology with which the book of Genesis opens. It is to distort seriously its great message if we try to make of it a barrier either to an evolutionary theory of creation or to the full equality of women in the sight of God.

Mrs. Stanton and the other suffragists were right in refusing to make Paul the final arbiter of their destinies. The Gospels reflect the experience and the memories of the early church. Yet the picture of Jesus shines through with great clarity—enough to make clear that he had no such sense of the inferiority of women as was

142

found in the surrounding Jewish culture and in some of
Paul's words. The often quoted words of Paul about
the silence and submission of women were not all he
said, and he probably did not write I Timothy. But
granted they reflect one side of his thinking, we have a
perfect right to differ with him. To fix on these as regu-
lative for all time is to distort and conceal more pro-
found and universal aspects of his writing. The tragedy
of the situation is that this has so often been done, and
is still occurring.

With these principles in mind, let us see what light
on the status of woman can be found in the first three
chapters of Genesis and in the New Testament. We must
try to avoid reading into the interpretation our own
prejudices, though in any such study this danger lurks
in the offing. I shall try to say what the relevant passages
convey of truth and situation-conditioned error in the
light of the best biblical scholarship I can discover.

2. *The first creation story*

Even a superficial look at the first three chapters of
Genesis shows that two different accounts of creation are
found there. The first extends from Genesis 1:1 through
2:4a; the second includes Genesis 2:4b–3:24. Why two?
And why the difference between them?

This leads immediately into the question of how the
Pentateuch, the first five books of the Bible, was written.
Without some knowledge of at least the outlines of this
process, we shall not be in a position to interpret cor-
rectly these first three chapters.

In the Pentateuch four strands of oral tradition and
written material are woven together, commonly referred
to as J, E, D, and P. The J, or Yahwist, strand (first

identified and named by German biblical scholarship) is so called because in it God is referred to as Yahweh, or Jahweh in German. It probably originated in the period of the United Kingdom during the reign of Solomon, about 950 B.C. or somewhat later. This originated in the South. In the Northern Kingdom around 750, another document came into being which goes by the name of E. This is so called because it refers to the deity as Elohim, a name not used in the early history of the Hebrews. About 700 some nameless editor wove these two accounts together. Later than this but prior to 621, another document was compiled, largely consisting of law codes but with narrative material interwoven (strand D). This constitutes mainly our book of Deuteronomy, or "second law," with the Deuteronomic Code which succeeds the Covenant Code of an earlier date. The finding of this document during the repair of the Temple at Jerusalem, perhaps put there to be found, prompted King Josiah's great reformation after Huldah the prophetess had declared it to be the authentic Word of God. During the period of the Exile a final edition of the historical part of Deuteronomy was compiled.

This brings us to the fourth strand, P, or the priestly document. It also was probably compiled in the Exile period, far from Jerusalem but not far from the worship of the Most High. It incorporates a sense of the majesty and holiness of God, and an atmosphere of worship pervades it. It contains meaningful symbolism and bears the marks of a long history of worship, which had not been lost but enriched in depth by separation from its former geographical center. Finally, a nameless editor arranged and combined these four accounts in what seemed to him the right consecutive order, to constitute what Jesus and Paul knew as the Torah and what we call the Pentateuch.[4]

The P document is of special concern to this study because it contains the account of the creation of the world, including the creation of male and female, with which the Bible begins, though it is the latest to be written. It is on a more sublime spiritual and cosmic level than J. Its account of the creation in six days is not scientific history. It takes only a casual observation to discover that, from a literal standpoint, there is something wrong with the creation of light and the production of vegetation and fruit trees before the sun and moon came into being. Attempts to defend its accuracy as science by claiming that the six days represent geological epochs, or the still more far-fetched defense by quoting Psalm 90:4, "A thousand years in thy sight are but as yesterday when it is past," serve only to make absurd both the creation story and such citations. Yet the utter sovereignty and holiness of God, and man's dignity and stewardship of the earth, shine through it with great clarity. It is in reality a great hymn of creation. The refrain after each day, "And God saw that it was good," coming to its climax and crescendo in "And God saw everything that he had made, and behold, it was very good," is a truth that ought never to be forgotten in a day of darkness and despair.

The P account of creation, written some four centuries after J, moves, as we shall see presently, on a high plane of both poetic beauty and spiritual insight. What does it say about women? The crucial words are found in Genesis 1:26-28.

Then God said, "Let us make man in our image, after our likeness; and let them have dominion over the fish of the sea, and over the birds of the air, and over the cattle, and over all the earth, and over every creeping thing that creeps upon the earth." So God created man in his own image, in the image of God he created him; male and female he created them. And God blessed them, and God said to them, "Be fruitful and multiply, and fill the earth and subdue it. . . ."

The reference to the fishes, birds, cattle, and other living things is clearly a brief suggestion of the many things included in "over all the earth." The fact that vastly more things are known now than then does not detract from the divine promise of "dominion," or from the divine injunction to responsible use of such stewardship. It has a bearing today upon ecology. But the heart of the problem now under consideration lies at two points: the meaning of man in this passage and the meaning of the image of God.

A short linguistic study gives an answer to the first question. The word used here for man is *adham,* which means man in the generic sense, not man as a male biological creature. Much confusion has arisen from the fact that the English language uses *man* in both senses, and to distinguish between the two meanings I shall temporarily refer to generic man as Man. As soon as we see that *adham* means Man, universal Man, any incongruity disappears from the statement, "In the image of God he created him; male and female he created them." The divine blessing and injunction to be fruitful and multiply, to fill the earth and subdue it, and to have dominion over other living things with divine provision for food from the earth to sustain them, apply as fully to female as to male.

This interpretation is reinforced a little further on where we read in Genesis 5:1-2, "When God created man, he made him in the likeness of God. Male and female he created them, and he blessed them and named them Man when they were created." Then immediately the term *adham* modulates into the name of Adam in the next verse, "When Adam had lived a hundred and thirty years, he became the father of a son in his own likeness, after his image, and named him Seth."

In the biblical passages the ambiguity as to whether the word translated *man* refers to one sex or two continues to be a source of misunderstanding. We have to judge from the context, and this is not always clear. It is awkward to try to spell it out with precision each time the term is used. However, sometimes this needs to be done in order to make it clear beyond any doubt that both men and women are equally made in the image of God, both receive the blessing of God, and both are commissioned by him to exercise creative dominion over his world. Let me give an example.

In my studies of the suffrage movement I came across an interesting observation on this point by Dr. Anna Howard Shaw. She took no part in the ill-fated *Woman's Bible*. But she was a graduate of Boston University School of Theology and knew well the generic meaning of *adham* in the first chapter of Genesis. She also had unusual skill in the use of language. This is how she met the problem we are now considering:

> He created man, male and female man, and called their name Adam, and to this male and female man, whom he called Adam, He gave all things, and bade this man Adam, male and female, to subdue all things, even the world, to themselves.[5]

No doubt this statement appeared to many as heretical as did the *Woman's Bible!* But it states unequivocally that in this crucial passage of the creation story about the origin of Man, both male and female were involved.

As for the making of Man in the image of God, there is more room for differences of opinion. Only the crudest literalism would take this to mean that God has a physical body with male sex organs after which a man's body is fashioned. Few would go this far, but the fact that throughout all Judeo-Christian history God has been referred to as "he" has inevitably left a residue of maleness in the thought of deity. I do not recommend that we now substitute "she" or "he-she" or "it"; either of the first two would be ridiculous and the third would carry an impersonal connotation altogether too prevalent today. Even to address the deity as "Father-Mother God," as I have heard it done, seems like straining the point further than is necessary. We have to use a pronoun, and "he" has the force of such a long tradition that there is no need now to alter our language. What is needed is to recognize that the masculine pronoun came to be used both for generic Man and for the deity because of an assumption, deeply embedded in human society, of the inherent superiority of the male. This is an assumption which the priestly creation story does not validate.

The image of God means that God has made Man with qualities akin to his own, and thus has conferred upon all persons, both male and female, a dignity and worth beyond anything else in the created world. With it he has given to mankind a great responsibility. Sometimes this has been conceived in terms of rationality; sometimes as dominion over the lower creation; sometimes as an original righteousness lost by the Fall and restored only by divine grace. It has been suggested

148

that Man is God's representative, somewhat as the image of a king represents and keeps in memory the king's majesty and power.[6]

All these views carry intimations of the meaning of the image of God, valuable in suggestiveness but prone to distortion if taken too exclusively. Without trying to limit the term too closely, we might better say that the personhood of Man, in a limited and finite way, is a reflection of the supreme personhood, or personality, of his Creator. Human personality we know, and where we find it at its best it is characterized by a loving concern for all other persons, a basic goodness, and a knitting together of wisdom with creativity in the kind of responsible action which man's freedom of choice and decision makes possible. Such qualities can be frightfully misused and lie undeveloped or be drained away, but they are the gift of the Creator to his highest creation. Is it not then reasonable to think of the Creator as possessing them in infinite measure, and imparting them to men and women made in his spiritual image?

A full discussion of the Judeo-Christian understanding of either Man or God is too large a subject for inclusion at this point. We shall come to it again in a later chapter. What concerns us now is the place of sex in the biblical creation stories and the bearing they have on the man-woman relation in our time.

That Man is a dual creation and that we are born either male or female through no choice of our own is a certainty amid all the uncertainties of human existence. This implies both *sexual difference* and *sexual partnership,* and we neglect or overlook either one of them at our peril. Human life is like most other living things in being bipolar, but sex in human existence carries with it both values and obligations far surpassing

149

anything to be found in the subhuman part of creation.

I do not agree with all that Karl Barth has said about the man-woman relationship, but he has put the matter accurately when he says that we have a double duty to live "as man *or* woman" and "as man *and* woman." [7] As creatures made in the divine image, we have many responsibilities in which there are no sexual differentiations except as society, rightly or wrongly, has set them for us. In other matters, our responsibilities are embedded in the fact of a dual sexuality in the created world of persons, and to defy or to attempt to obliterate these differences is to court disaster for ourselves and for those whose lives we touch.

A note which needs to be held in the foreground of the woman's movement of our time is adumbrated in the simple words, "male and female he created them." No superiority of status is implied in these words, or can be drawn out of them without distortion. Yet a basic sex distinction is affirmed. Many more opportunities for service in economic, civic, and church life ought to be opened up to women; yet those exponents of the Women's Liberation Movement who seem to be trying virtually to become unsexed are not only thwarting nature but creating barriers for the movement. Nothing is gained when a man becomes effeminate, or when a woman tries to renounce her femininity. What is needed is to accept one's sex, whichever it may be, without rebellion against God or fate, and to find within it one's fullest personhood.

2. *The second creation story*

We must turn now to the J or Yahwist story of creation and Man's first disobedience. Not only is this account much earlier, but it bears more traces of a highly personal mythology. The author of the priestly account was doubtless familiar with the J strand. The fact that he chose to write his own interpretation of creation suggests that he believed there was more to be said.

The creation story of Genesis 2:4a through the end of chapter three is less majestic than the priestly account with which the Bible opens, but it makes its contribution if we understand why it was written. The storyteller was trying to answer several important questions about human nature—its source, its intended destiny, why it has fallen away from its God-given purpose, why there should be both male and female persons, why men have to work and women must bear children, both amid difficulty and pain. He did not succeed in giving complete answers, but he gave the interpretation that seemed most plausible to his thinking and that of his time. If we can take it for what it is— an ancient myth with spiritual overtones and a sense of the moral as well as the cosmic ultimacy of the Creator, it can teach us something. We lose its most essential notes if we take it as history and as a text for the subordination of women. To center attention on Eve's responsibility for Adam's sin, or to find in it authorization for a doctrine of original sin on which to erect a mammoth structure of ecclesiastical procedures, is seriously to misread it.

Taken as a whole, the Yahwist narrative is a remarkable literary achievement. With a great sweep through Israel's early history, it celebrates the mighty acts of Yahweh by which he led the covenant community, his chosen people, out of bondage in Egypt and through the trials of the wilderness and into the Promised Land, all this in spite of repeated infractions of their side of the covenant. The narrative falls into three main sections: first, chapters two through eleven with the stories of the Garden of Eden, Cain and Abel, Noah and the flood, and the tower of Babel; second, the patriarchal period through the remainder of Genesis; and third, Israel's life story from the Exodus to the Conquest in the rest of the Pentateuch into Joshua.

We can deal here only with the beginning of it. But it is important to see that the Garden of Eden story does not stand alone but is written as a sort of preface; that it is mythology and myth with a meaning; and that this mythological preface is an attempt to answer some of man's enduring questions. That is, it is etiological in its purpose rather than cosmological as is the first creation story.

The J account begins with the creation of man from the ground (adamah). This is a play on words with adham but may suggest the good earth from which Man must draw his sustenance. But Man is not simply dirt; he is the creation of Yahweh whose breath (spirit) animates the dust to make it a living being. The older version read "a living soul," but to the Hebrew mind there was no dichotomy of soul and body. Then comes the garden with its pleasant foliage and fruit, and the tree of life and the tree of knowledge.

Bypassing a bit of ancient geography, we come to the man's commission to till and tend the garden, eating anything he desires except the fruit of the tree of the knowledge of good and evil. Are we to suppose that God did not want this man, or any man, to know good from evil? Hardly, for without some such knowledge there would be no responsible choice or decision. The key to the injunction comes in Genesis 3:5, where it is indicated that when the man ate the forbidden fruit,

152

he desired in his presumption to be "like God." In view of the danger of "playing God" in an advanced technological society, it is not difficult to draw a homily from this passage if we do not distort it.

But the crux of the story from the standpoint of our present inquiry comes in Genesis 2:21-24 with the creation of woman and the establishment of the marriage relation. After the cattle, the birds, and the beasts of the field had been created, still "for the man there was not found a helper fit for him." The creation of Eve from the rib of Adam in the first recorded obstetrical sleep is a story too familiar to require retelling. In the most intimate of all unions they become one flesh.

There is by no means agreement as to the correct translation of what the Revised Standard Version renders as "a helper fit for him." The sexes are clearly differentiated—*ish* and *ishshah,* but what is the relation of the *ishshah* to the *ish*? The King James version has "a help meet for him," from which comes the word "helpmeet" or "helpmate" referring primarily to a wife, but also to a co-worker or companion. The Moffatt translation tells us that after all the animals had been shaped from the ground and named, "no helper could be found to suit man himself." A German commentary (Delitzsch) says, "a mirror of himself, in which he recognizes himself." Perhaps most satisfactory of all is the plain English of the New English Bible, "Then the Lord God said, 'It is not good for the man to be alone. I will provide a partner for him.' "

Such partnership along with a sexual difference we found to be implied in the priestly story of creation, as an essential note in the belief that Man is made in the image of God. This is reinforced here if we take the NEB translation. In any case, it is basic to human existence, at all times including the present. Unless the man and woman of today find a satisfying partnership, whether in the home or in other human relations, unhappiness and conflict are bound to be the result. But the term "helper" carries no opprobrium when it does not suggest servitude. Many women prefer to be called homemakers rather than housewives, and one of them hit the nail on the head when she said that she married a husband, not a house!

Nevertheless, I do not think that we can absolve the J author from the assumption that women were created for the sake of men. Do what we will with the rib story, it carries this implication. It is corroborated by Adam's blaming Eve for his transgression in eating the forbidden fruit instead of assuming his own responsibility. Instead of a manly protectiveness, there seems to be an attempt to hide behind—not her skirts as yet but a leafy apron. From this part of the story a long tradition, not yet ended, arose which makes woman the temptress in sexual affairs, and this is one source of the idea of a celibate clergy. Furthermore, the prediction of Genesis 3:16, "he shall rule over you," has many times been quoted as justification for the subordination of women in family, church, and society in general.

The outcome of the story is that a curse is placed upon all the players in this drama: the serpent becomes the enemy of Man, the woman must bear children in pain while her husband rules over her, the man must earn bread in the sweat of his brow until he returns to the dust from which he came. And both human figures, their pristine innocence ended, are exiled forever from their garden of delight.

If we take this as a primitive explanation of sex, of sin, and of suffering, with a sovereign God the source of all creation and Man a responsible creature who disobeys the divine will at his peril, the story is great drama which carries some vital theological insights. If we take it as literal history, it reinforces both male dominance and female seductiveness. This it has continued to do through the centuries, though perhaps less as the source of the idea of male superiority than as an argument for an already existing social pattern.

The idea of original sin or the fall from a state of original righteousness in the innocence of Paradise has long been attached to the story. Paul made use of it in this manner by contrasting Adam the sinner with Christ the savior. "For as in Adam all die, so also in Christ shall all be made alive (I Cor. 15:22). However, we should note that the Old Testament does not make this deduction. There is sin on almost every page of the Old Testament, and its great theme is the blending of judgment with the steadfast love of God for his erring people. But the sin is not attributed to Adam, and save for Paul's use of it in this context, the doctrine of original sin would not have become embedded in Christian theology.

To return to our main theme, we noted that the Genesis stories of creation carry a twofold emphasis on sexual difference and sexual partnership. This is more evident in P than in J but present even there if "helper" is translated as a "partner". What does this mean today?

According to this ancient story, the man is ordained to be the breadwinner and the woman the childbearer of the family and of the race. This remains, under conditions greatly changed from the time when J was compiled, the normal state of affairs. Exceptions must be made, for today many women must support not only themselves but their dependents, and marriage and

155

motherhood are not universally taken for granted. Yet the functions of the sexes set forth in the Yahwist story continue to be major functions. Grounded at least as far as women are concerned in biological structure, and to a lesser degree in the superior muscular strength of the male, it seems not too far-fetched to say that they are divinely ordained.

But is this a curse? Not if there is partnership. Without such partnership, strains develop in the nuclear family which too often lead to its final collapse. The wife is not the only homemaker, the husband is also. Likewise, in the larger family of human society the partnership of women with men in business and the professions, in government and politics, in education and in the churches, is required for the fullest functioning in any of these pursuits.

The breadwinning of the male and the childbearing of the female are important obligations, not to be treated lightly. But they are not the only obligations of either sex. If they are made into exclusive pursuits, there is a distortion of the partnership. In many spheres of human activity, men and women can fruitfully cooperate. But while this basic truth is being emphasized, as it needs to be in our time, the other side of it must not be lost. If sexual differences are disregarded to the point where women disclaim their femininity and men their male responsibilities, everybody loses.

4. *In the New Testament*

I shall speak more briefly of the status of women in the New Testament, for a large part of chapter three was devoted to this theme. There we saw the difference between the attitude of Jesus and that of his contemporaries, and noted the ambivalence of Paul's attitude toward the women of the early church. However, some further considerations need to be included in the picture.

Throughout the Old Testament and intertestamental period, women remained in a subordinate position. As indicated earlier, there are narratives about exceptional women, such as Miriam and Deborah, Ruth and Naomi, Vashti and Esther. At the end of the book of Proverbs there is a fine tribute to "the virtuous woman." A woman could be honored as the bearer of sons and the guardian of her household, but she must permit her male lord to rule over her.

To appreciate fully the attitude of Jesus toward women as persons, we must compare it with the degree to which women were looked down upon in rabbinical Judaism.

One should not converse with a woman, not even with one's own wife; women are greedy eaters, curious listeners, indolent, jealous, and frivolous; "many women, much witchcraft"; "ten cabs of garrulousness descended upon the world, nine came down upon the women, one upon the rest of the world." "Blessed is he whose children are male and woe to him whose children are female"—in the light of the attitude toward women expressed in these quotations this outcry of ben Kiddushin is understandable.[8]

In the synagogues which replaced the Temple worship in the dispersion of the Jews, the women were not only separated from the men but were required to sit behind screens if they attended at all. The Jerusalem Talmud says that the Torah should rather be burned than transmitted to women. Thus women were excluded largely from the religious as well as the social life of the times of Jesus.

In the light of such a setting, the fact that Jesus even spoke with women takes on the proportions of a remarkable challenge to the *status quo*. It gives meaning to the reaction of the disciples after he had talked with the Samaritan woman at the well, "They marveled that he was talking with a woman" (John 4:27). In doing so he disregarded both the written and the unwritten laws of his community. When we add to this the numerous cases in which he healed women and praised their fidelity, no specific words of his are required to demonstrate his belief in the equality of women. That a band of women should have accompanied the journeys of Jesus and the twelve disciples (Luke 8:2-3), should have stood at the foot of the cross and were witnesses to the resurrection, as all four of the Gospels indicate, and should have been present later in the upper room with the eleven remaining disciples (Acts 1:14), must have seemed utterly shocking to the contemporaries of Jesus. I need not restate what has been said earlier of such evidences of the attitude of Jesus, but it is important to see it both in contrast with his Jewish heritage and in relation to a new note which he injected into the stream of Christian thought.

We have also looked previously at the attitudes of Paul, and have summed them up by saying that as a Jew in the Greek world he was opposed to any speaking or assumption of leadership by women in the young churches, while as a Christian he had a very warm feeling toward the women who were working and witnessing in these same churches. As a situation-conditioned male he had an outlook quite different from that of Jesus, but as a Christian he had caught the spirit of Jesus to the point where he could say, "There is neither Jew nor Greek, there is neither slave nor free, there is neither male nor female; for you are all one in Christ Jesus."

Since the position of women in the family is a vital part of the total Christian outlook, let us look further at what both Jesus and Paul said on this subject. Little is recorded of the words of Jesus on it except his definite rejection of divorce. Even the concession found in the Gospel of Matthew but not Mark, "except for unchastity," is regarded by most scholars as a later interpolation. But he was thoroughly familiar with the Genesis stories of creation and quoted from them. In reply to the query, "Is it lawful to divorce one's wife for any cause?" his reply blends quotations from Genesis 1:27 and Genesis 2:24, "Have you not read that he who made them from the beginning made them male and female, and said, 'For this reason a man shall leave his father and mother and be joined to his wife, and the two shall become one'? So they are no longer two but one. What therefore God has joined together, let not man put asunder" (Matt. 19:4-6). Although in today's world this should not be taken as a legalistic prescription for all time, what it reflects of the solemnity of the marriage relation ought never to be lost.

Paul says many more words on the subject. In a rather extended discussion of marriage in the seventh chapter of I Corinthians, he makes it clear that he is single and thinks highly of this estate, but "because of the temptation to immorality, each man should have his own wife and each woman her own husband" (I Cor. 7:2). He counsels the unmarried and widows to stay single as he is, but gives an unromantic reason for marriage in words which the King James Version puts as bluntly as it can be stated, "But if they cannot contain, let them marry: for it is better to marry than to burn" (vs. 9). The Revised Standard Version softens it to "to be aflame with passion." This has sometimes concealed the fact that in between these verses Paul is very reasonable, very equalitarian, in what he says about sex relations within marriage. Each should give the other their conjugal rights; neither partner rules over his own body, and each should submit to the other. Apparently he did not wish to see marriages break up on grounds of sexual incompatibility.

But let us look again at what he says about women, and note the dual strain that runs through his thinking. In I Corinthians 11:3 he makes the startling statement, "But I want you to understand that the head of every man is Christ, the head of a woman is her husband, and the head of Christ is God." In such a hierarchy, there is nothing for a woman to do but to let her husband be her lord and master! This is reinforced a little further on by an allusion to the rib story, "For man was not made from woman, but woman from man. Neither was man created for woman, but woman for man" (I Cor. 11:8-9). Here is clearly a male deduction. But Paul seems not to have been content to leave it at that. His Christian conscience was at work, and he interrupts his dictum on the need for women to wear veils in church to speak a word on the need for mutuality and partnership. "Nevertheless, in the Lord woman is not independent of man nor man of woman; for as woman was made from man, so man is now born of woman. And all things are from God" (I Cor. 11:11-12).

In Colossians also there is an important passage in much the same mood. In Colossians 3:11 there is an echo of Galatians 3:28, though without a specific reference to women. Several verses further on we find Paul saying, "Wives, be subject to your husbands, as is fitting in the Lord. Husbands, love your wives, and do not be harsh with them" (Col. 3:18-19). The intervening verses contain injunctions to compassion, kindness, patience, forbearance, and forgiveness, and these virtues are summed up in the words, "And above all these put on love, which binds everything together in perfect harmony" (Col. 3:14). Apparently Paul believed that such qualities should characterize the life of the Christian, in the marriage relation as elsewhere, but he could not bring himself to affirm the equality of wives with husbands.

This is enough to illustrate the ambivalence of Paul's thinking in relation to the place of women in the family, as we have earlier noted it in relation to the church. On the one hand, a long tradition reinforced by the second creation story in Genesis made woman seem to him definitely "the second sex." On the other, Paul could feel deeply the force of Christian love. Jesus had a higher estimate of the dignity and worth of women as persons. But the weight of social tradition and the influence of the adverse side of Paul's teaching have submerged this insight. The time is ripe for a clearer vision and reappraisal.

VII Sex and continuous creation

The preceding chapter has dealt with certain barriers unnecessarily but frequently drawn from the Bible. The Bible is an important source of Christian theology, but it is not the only source. As was indicated previously, the Christian faith takes its origin not only from the Bible but from the living stream of Christian experience, and unless we are to deny any validity to natural theology, it is shaped also by an examination of the total structure of the world. The last is particularly important in a scientific age, for while science cannot replace theology—both are distorted if we attempt this—a factual inquiry into the nature of the world as we find it can provide valuable light as to the nature of the ultimate or governing Power that shapes its existence.

The time is ripe for an attempt to formulate a theology of sex to include the man-woman relationship as a whole. Has not this often been done? There is no dearth of books which deal with sex as a biological function, and not only the psychology and the sociology but the theology of the marriage relation has been explored. But this is not all there is of sex. In the spate of books and articles which have appeared since the Women's Liberation Movement became a popular concern, the interest appears to be almost entirely sociological. Among earlier treatments the only book I have found which deals helpfully with the theological angle of the problem is D. S. Bailey's *Sexual Relation in*

Christian Thought,[1] and the author's concern is almost wholly with the history of Christian thought on the subject. He has one chapter on the theology of sex to which I am indebted, and there are brief references in other books, but what I shall now attempt to say must for the most part be carved out independently.

1. *The structure of creation*

There are four aspects of the wider range of Christian theology which relate directly to our subject. The first of these is the meaning and structure of creation. This calls into consideration whatever there may be that is of special importance in the man-woman relation, and in particular in the creation of woman as a female being. The second is the Christian understanding of Man. Here we must consider the bearing of a Christian view of Man on that half of mankind that is other than man in the physiological sense. The third is the Christian doctrine of redemption. This must on the surface seem irrelevant to a study of the sexes, for there is nearly universal agreement among Christians that salvation through Jesus Christ is open to both men and women. But because Jesus was a male, it has long and often been argued that only males may fitly represent him in his church as mediators of salvation. A fourth and broad issue lies in the field of theological ethics and the Christian's social responsibilities, insofar as they have a bearing on the man-woman relation. These concerns are much interwoven with one another but can be looked at one after the other. We shall consider the first three at some length with intimations of the fourth.

We begin, then, with the structure of creation and the place of sex within it. But what is sex? Words change meaning with time and usage. One dictionary defines sex as "the physical difference between male and female animals; the possession of reproductive organs of a particular kind; differentiation in the functions of the reproductive organs." This seems to be as accurate a biological definition as could be framed. But another dictionary at least leaves open the possibility that more than biology is involved, "the distinction between male and female, or that property or character by which an animal is male or female." Neither of these definitions takes into account vast differences between the human and subhuman world of sex.

If we limit attention now to the human sphere, popular usage has almost restricted sex to the physical elements of sexual union. There are frequent references to "sex experience," to movies, dramas, or literature that are "sexy," or simply to "having sex" in marriage or in extramarital unions. Even "sex education" relates mainly, though fortunately not exclusively, to the biology and physiology of human reproduction rather than to the wider aspects of personal existence as male or female. Just as the adjective "immoral" or a "morals charge" against an offender has taken on the connotation of a physical infraction of the social code in regard to sexual behavior, so "sexual intercourse" is limited to its physiological meaning. If we could start from scratch in the use of terminology, sexual intercourse ought to mean the widest possible relationship of mind and spirit between men and women in a social context, whether educational, economic, political, psychological, cultural, or religious. But we cannot thus affix meanings at will to terms which have acquired other meanings, and we shall probably have to go on speaking about sexual intercourse as if it meant coitus, and that only. Yet important as this is, it is not all there is of sex in the man-woman relationship.

In this discussion I shall not be dealing primarily with coitus. Enough others have done that. I wish the reader to think with me of sex in the total structure of creation as Man exists in the man-woman relation, male and female. Various observations along this line were made in the previous chapter, but since the Bible is not the only source of a theology of creation, there is more to be said.

Christian theology has traditionally held to a doctrine of creation *ex nihilo*, out of nothing, as if originally there was a complete blank, then suddenly "in the beginning" God created the heavens and the earth. This originated from the Genesis story of creation. But even after the geological history of the earth and the evolution of man from lower forms of life became generally accepted, it could still be held that evolution began by divine fiat at some point in time, and so also the creation of the world. This is not the usual scientific position, but it has sometimes been defended scientifically, and not in jest as the term might suggest, by the "big bang" theory of the origin of the earth and probably also of the other planets and the rest of the solar system.

Such a creation all at once is not the prevailing mood of theology today. Much attention is now being given to "process theology," which owes a special debt to Alfred North Whitehead and to Charles Hartshorne, and is persuasively being advocated by theologians like John Cobb, Jr., Norman Pittenger, and others. Its central note is a continuous creation. This is not a new idea, for it was being advocated by the liberal theology of a half-century ago. However, process theology adds important nuances of thought in a complete rejection of creation *ex nihilo,* the substitution of a continuous interaction of the world with God in a mutual, organic relation of each to the other, and consequently the rejection of divine omnipotence as coercive power. Following Whitehead, it reinterprets the power of God as persuasion, tenderness, and creative love. This relieves considerably the theoretical difficulties in the problem of evil by absolving God of responsibility for causing everything to happen just as it does.

I find much to commend in process theology, though at times it seems to me to skate perilously close to making God the demiurge of Plato's *Timaeus,* not the creator but the architect or fashioner of the world. The peril is not to truth if this view be the true one, but to the ultimacy of God, and this has always been a main tenet of Christian theology. I too believe in a continuous creation in which God is not the arbitrary determiner of all human destiny including its evil aspects. But I also believe in a God of infinite wisdom, goodness, and power who has, in his wisdom and goodness, limited his power to coerce the course of events. These limitations appear in certain basic processes and forces of creation without which we could not exist as persons—the orderliness of nature, the responsible freedom of man, and the network of social relations within which we live and without which we should perish. In such a world, God and man must work together to create a world conforming more nearly to God's will and purpose.

I do not think we know, or can know, whether this process had a beginning in time. This lies outside the range of any evidence. Certainly *Man* had a beginning in his emergence from the subhuman level of animate life; probably the earth did, whether by the "big bang" process or otherwise. This is for science, not theology, to determine. But when it comes to the ultimate origins of the total created universe, either a world with a beginning or a world coeternal with God is acceptable to Christian thought, provided God is still the Ultimate One.

The biblical account of creation gives no complete answer to the question of the manner of God's creative process, for while Genesis 1:1 uses the term, "In the beginning . . . , Genesis 1:2 speaks of God's Spirit brooding over a dark, formless, watery abyss to bring light and order to it. On the creation *ex nihilo* question, Walter M. Horton some years ago wrote:

The Christian Fathers declared that God created the world "out of nothing"; i.e., neither out of his own divine substance nor out of any sort of pre-existent stuff. This view does not commit Christian thought to any crudely anthropomorphic or magical conception of God's creative power—as though the Creator snapped his fingers and cried Abracadabra!—nor does it profess to offer any intelligible explanation of the creative process; it simply declares that the stuff as well as the structure of the world has God for its Author.[2]

I am content to leave the origin of creation at that, provided we are entitled to believe that God is continually at work within his world and that in this process he has called us to be his servants. I believe, furthermore, that we are entitled to believe with the ancient seer who wrote the first chapter of Genesis that this is a *good* world. Yet there are recalcitrant evil elements in it which God has commissioned us to "subdue" and to eradicate, to the end that the more abundant life for all may prevail.

Before we move to a specific application of this view

167

of a continuous creation to a theology of sex, some other angles of it require attention. One of them is the need to emphasize that while God is vastly more than his world, he is present at all times within it. In other words, God is both transcendent to and immanent within his world. He does not come into the world by occasional interventions, though his presence is at times more visible than at other times. Since God is in the total creative process, it will not do to make too sharp a differentiation between the human and divine elements in it. Both biblical and much popular thought assume that what Man does God does not do, and vice versa. The net result is that as human knowledge and achievement advance, God is crowded to the fringes. Thus, to many minds in the current secularization of society, God is entirely excluded.

The philosophical form of the view that God is completely transcendent to the world, having created it but left it to its own initiative, is deism. Its opposite is pantheism, which in its extreme forms equates God with the world. God may then survive as a cosmic religious vision and reverence for all existence, but not as having any personal relation to individual persons or to the events that affect their living. Since persons and particular events must be taken into account because they impinge so directly upon us, God disappears by this route as readily as by the deistic approach. A modified form of the denial of divine transcendence does not equate God with everything that exists, but with human impulses toward good in the attempt to set at right a disordered world. It is on this basis that the "radical theology" of our time defends a form of "Christian atheism," which closely resembles what used to be known as humanism.

168

To avoid these extremes, it appears to me essential to hold to both the transcendence and the immanence of God, and to a world which depends for its existence on such a deity. In the world, God is actively at work in all that occurs but does not coerce the course of events to stifle human initiative or set aside the orderly processes of nature. History then becomes an ongoing process in which there is much thwarting of the divine purpose, but also a forward movement in which God and Man are working together to create a better world or, in biblical language, to advance the kingdom of God. In this enterprise, both men and women have an opportunity and an obligation.

A further angle of continuous creation is the need to emphasize the reality of potentials. In one sense, what is potential but not yet actual is unreal. But in another sense, we leave out the main thrust of both divine purpose and human goals if we fail to reckon with the power of such purposes and goals to bring the potential into actuality. To illustrate, when Jesus was born he must have resembled any other little Jewish boy baby. Yet the whole picturesque beauty of the Christmas story centers in the belief that God had a special mission for him to fulfill. It is not to question the uniqueness of Jesus to say that in a comparable sense every child, male or female, has God-given potentialities which the parents, the child himself as he grows to maturity, and the wider society must strive to bring to fulfillment.

2. Identity and difference

This outline of what is implied by continuous creation has necessarily been stated in somewhat general terms. But we must now look carefully at an important question which has heretofore been intentionally bypassed. This is the matter of distinctive differences in male and female personality which can be traced to the biological structure of human creation.

I have emphasized throughout this book the importance of sex equality in human society. But equality by no means connotes identity. The Declaration of Independence states, "We hold these truths to be self-evident, that all men are created equal." Certainly neither Thomas Jefferson nor any signer of the Declaration believed that all men are created exactly alike; this would not "be self-evident" but obviously untrue. What they were contending for was the "unalienable" right of all to life, liberty, and the pursuit of happiness. It is these rights in a contemporary form which are now being contended for in protests against the subordination of women as an inferior half of the human race.

In the structure of creation there are certain obvious differences between male and female persons. Besides the difference in genitals detectable at birth, boy babies usually grow into men who are larger than women and have greater muscular strength. For this reason, there are some things men can do which women ought not to try to do. Girls develop into women who can bear children—the one endowment women have which no man possesses. There are other minor differences such as the tonal quality of voice, a woman's fuller bust, and a man's hairy beard.

Beyond these basic physiological differences, whatever male or female characteristics appear in adult life can be traced very largely to social conditioning rather than to innate propensities. This is a field in which there is no full agreement, since the conditioning begins very early to modify the newly created person, but the weight of evidence lies in this direction.

But first let us look back to the childhood of the race. As far in the past as there is any historical evidence, women, because they bore children, had to stay close at home, tending the family fires as well as the children, cooking the meat which the hunter-husband brought home, and tilling plots of ground nearby. We saw that agriculture probably began this way. Meanwhile, the husband was free to roam where he would, and where he must if he was either to ward off enemies or be successful in the hunt. Already, even before grain was raised to make bread, he was the breadwinner of the family and the woman the childbearer and keeper of the home.

There is no need to trace this process through the nomadic, agricultural, and industrial stages of civilization to see that these remained the dual roles of male and female. If women had been more free to leave their homes, the whole course of civilization might have been different. Yet because of their reproductive role in the order of creation, they were not free. Not until the last two centuries did they even think that they might be free, and this whole matter is still in flux. To the extent that satisfying employment outside the home is available to women, birth control is practiced, and the right of women to remain unmarried without social stigma is acknowledged, there is inevitably a quest for freedom from ancient roles. Add to these situations the wider education of women and a longer life with twenty or thirty good years after the youngest child has left home, and it would be surprising if women did not wish to add a further vocation to that of motherhood.

This new freedom by no means implies that women

can, or should, surrender their God-given function as mothers, or that men except for temporary or special reasons should be content to let their wives support them. These functions are grounded in the order of a continuing creation, and hence may be thought to be within the design of God in the creation of the sexes. Nor do I think that most women, or most men, have any strong desire to evade these responsibilities. What women object to is the limitation of their roles to motherhood and homemaking to the exclusion or disparagement of everything else.

But beyond these biological functions, almost everything in the matter of sex distinctions can be traced to social conditioning. Let us look now at the new baby as this child comes to birth from the procreative act of the parents and, theologically speaking, from the creative act of God in bringing into existence a new person. The sex organs already determine to a large extent the course the new life will take in later years. But this is far in the future. If the sex is not what one or both parents strongly desired, this may be an adverse factor from the beginning. But assuming that the child is joyously welcomed, what then?

Whether this child is a boy or a girl, the baby is equally lovable and equally troublesome. One sex is as adorable and cuddly as the other; each cries as much and must have all forms of attention as regularly. When the child begins to show signs of developing a personality, each responds as warmly to affection, and each as readily uses not only wails but little fists to fight back if thwarted.

However, it is not long before social conditioning begins. "Little boys don't play with dolls." "Little girls don't play with trains, or airplanes, or guns." Little

172

girls are attired in pretty dresses, all frills and femininity. Little boys are more soberly dressed in pants. A boy's pretty curls are soon cut off so that he will not look girlish, though a few years later it may become mannish, or at least modish, for him to have long hair. A girl's hair is dressed prettily and becomes the norm in the beauty ads for the glistening softness a woman's hair is supposed to have if the right product is used. All along the way, in a thousand unconscious ways, these children are being taught the difference between a boy's life and that of a girl.

By the time the child reaches the first grade in school, or even kindergarten, the differentiation is quite firmly set. It is not long before boys feel, with some encouragement from their elders as well as their peers, that it is manly to fight but not to cry, while girls learn to get what they want by tears. As maturity advances, the fist-fights may give way to profanity, and to the tears are added seductive wiles. I am reminded of the son of a friend who, with a more acute analysis than he was aware of, lamented that he was too old to cry but too young to swear.

As the boy or the girl child moves on to adolescence and to maturity, strong biological impulses assert themselves, and mating results. This is clearly a sexual attribute, designed in the nature of creation for an affinity of the sexes that will result in the reproduction of the race. We shall bypass for the present the host of problems related to it. Unlike subhuman animal mating, it calls for much responsible choice and decision on the part of the two immediately involved and the surrounding society.

What must be emphasized in this connection has a double thrust. On the one hand, there are deep and in-

173

eradicable differences between the sexes. Emil Brunner rightly says that "this distinction goes down to the very roots of our personal existence, and penetrates into the very deepest 'metaphysical' grounds of our personality and destiny." [3] In relation to the Christian doctrine of creation we may say also that this differentiation is a great good, with those of each sex having important functions to perform. Yet though it may seem contradictory to this first affirmation, observation reveals that virtually every sexual difference in adult life except the female's childbearing and the male's superior size and strength is the result of what society has done in shaping the individual's personality from birth to adulthood.

If these two principles can be accepted together and held in mutual self-correction, as too often they are not, important deductions follow. The first of these—the importance of combining sexual difference with sexual partnership in a complementary relation—was stressed in the previous chapter. Though it is entirely legitimate for women to do some things formerly done by men, and vice versa, nothing is gained when women try to deny their sex and act like men. Too much of the Women's Liberation Movement of the present seems to proceed on this basis. It is less common, in spite of fantastic dress and hair styles, for men to try to act like women, but where it occurs it is equally regrettable.

A second observation is that the time has come to put aside—let us hope, for ever—the superstition that women are less intelligent than men. There are plenty of scientific data to refute this notion. Some persons have even maintained that women have less intelligence because their brains are smaller! This is refuted on two counts: (1) in proportion to bodily size, the average female brain is a little larger than the male, and (2) no correlation whatever has been found to exist between human brain size and intelligence.[4] But a far more important factor is the use one is able to make of one's native intelligence. The intelligence tests and scholastic aptitude tests corroborate the observation of anyone who has ever taught boys and girls in the same class; namely, that neither sex is brighter than the other. However, what is tested cannot be wholly separated from previous experience and greater interest in the field, and these factors readily tip the scales of achievement in one direction or another.

Yet there is the incontrovertible fact that most of the great intellectual leaders of mankind have been men. Does this mean that, although women may have intelligence, they lack genius? Ashley Montagu in his interesting but possibly exaggerating book, *The Natural Superiority of Women,* answers this question succinctly in three stages: "Among the principal reasons why women do not have as many achievements to their credit as men are the following: (1) for the greater part of their history most fields of achievement have been closed to them; (2) in fields in which women were admitted they were not permitted to enter on an equal footing with men; (3) or, having been admitted, they were not encouraged to excel, were actively discouraged, or were not noticed at all." [5]

The emotional differences between men and women are a more intricate matter. The tendency to cry in times of deep distress or of joy is a matter of social conditioning. Other characteristics are more difficult to trace. Men are often said to be the more aggressive, hardheaded, and skilled in leadership, while women in addition to being more retiring are credited with being more compassionate, tenderhearted, and interested in personal relations. After due allowance has been made for the fact that there are aggressive women and compassionate men, there is some realism in this distinction as it appears in male and female experience. But is this due to creation or to culture? The sources come blended in the fact that the man's freedom to leave home and his responsibility for family support and protection have made him more experienced in the combativeness of public life. The woman's more restricted sphere and the need not only to bear but to rear her children and to protect her husband have tended to develop her natural maternal feelings along lines of loving concern and an interest in the details of personal living.

I shall mention only one further difference between the sexes, clearly rooted in biology though with social consequences. Women live longer than men. All the actuarial statistics attest this, and annuities are figured on this expectation. The theory used to be that men, because they work harder, wear themselves out more quickly. This is a doubtful premise. Studies in the biology of reproduction have given a more scientific reason. To put a complicated matter as simply as possible, women have two X chromosomes as carriers of sexual characteristics; men have an X and a Y chromosome with about an equal number of X and Y in the sperm. In union with the ovum, the X's create a new XX and the Y's a new XY. This potent additional X chromosome is the basic physiological reason why women have more resistance to disease, deteriorate physically less early, and thus live longer. Are women then "the weaker sex"? It depends on whether the measure is muscular strength or a constitutional capacity for endurance.

3. Contemporary changes

From what has been presented thus far, there is truth, though not the whole truth, in the statement of Simone de Beauvoir in *The Second Sex* that "one is not born, but rather becomes, a woman." [6] Sex, then, in either man or woman is essentially an effect of the environment. As a girl is shaped in childhood and then grows up, social pressures mold her into a "feminine creature" who has no autonomous being or meaning of her own. It is this false idea of femininity from which women must be liberated.

The truth in this view, from the standpoint of belief in a continuous creation, lies in the large amount of influence which environment and social expectations exert, for better or for worse, on both male and female characteristics. If what has been said earlier of the interaction of the divine and the human in the shaping of destiny is a sound position, women are what they are today by social pressures and not wholly by God's design. But the untruth in the environmental view lies in the fact that women in a crucial respect are different from men—"in the beginning" if there was a beginning, and in the creation of each new male or female child. The complementary differences between the sexes had better be accepted as God's gift rather than rebelled against.

Yet creation continues, and some significant changes, mainly for the better, are taking place in our time. Let us look at some of them.

The most important one of these changes is that women are no longer content to let chivalry, or such remnants of it as remain, take the place of basic social justice. Some women enjoy chivalry while others dislike

177

the idea of being placed on a pedestal in certain social matters. I myself should hate to see chivalry and the amenities of politeness disappear from the male sex! They harm nobody and are good for both men and women. But what is being demanded today, with a rising chorus that is not likely to be stifled by argument, disdain, or laughter, is that women be no longer regarded as inferior beings by reason of their sex.

This change of attitude from submission to a demand for equality of opportunity has been furthered by all the other major revolutions of our time, as was indicated in the first chapter of this book. Among the most potent forces have been a more widespread education of women, particularly along professional lines, a more conspicuous demonstration of the skills of women and their ability to make important contributions not only in the home but in public life, greater social acceptance of contraception to curtail the need of childbearing and of divorce to increase both the opportunity and the need of self-support, a greater need for two salaries in a home to meet the rising costs of the children's education and a more comfortable standard of living for all. Whether we like it or not, these trends are with us and are likely to increase rather than recede.

These factors are obvious, but there are less vital and still significant changes. What shall we make of the fact that male and female attire is no longer the distinguishing mark of sex? Particularly in a crowd of adolescent boys and girls, the distinguishing marks recede except for beards and mustaches. That women should take to slacks and pantsuits is explainable on the ground of greater freedom of movement. It is only in the burning of bras and other such far-out protests that there is any special linkage with the new feminism. But why have young men taken to long hair, beads, and often startling attire? The most obvious reason is the desire of many to defy the Establishment, and of others to follow the fashion set by their peers. Yet it may also be an indication that the young, whether male or female, will no longer countenance the sex discrimination of the ages.

This conclusion is borne out by the fact that many colleges which formerly were for men or for women only have of late become coeducational. The sexes clearly desire each other's company on a day-to-day basis. Furthermore, within the colleges co-ed dormitories are increasingly in vogue. These changes seem not to have increased sexual promiscuity, as many had feared, but to promote a healthier and more normal relationship between the sexes.

Another aspect of change in the mores of today, less healthy and less commendable, is an increase in the frequency or at least in the social acceptance of sexual intercourse outside marriage. It is less healthy because it erodes self-discipline, tends to make sex a matter of pleasurable indulgence rather than a high spiritual relationship, disregards both social standards and social consequences, and decreases the chances of a happy marriage in lasting fidelity. Yet with it has come some breaking down of the double standard of former days. It is still true that often "the woman pays" with an unwanted pregnancy, but there is less tendency than formerly to let the male slip away into anonymous oblivion.

There are other subtle indications of a change in the mores. It was quite customary for the women of an earlier day, under severe emotional shock or perhaps simply as a means of getting attention, to swoon. When have you seen a girl faint under such circumstances? In fact, women often seem to bear up better under trouble than men, and many a woman has felt the responsibility of remaining strong in order to sustain her husband in the shattering events of our time.

In the most violent and shattering of all pursuits, the waging of war, there are still sexual differences. Men but not women are drafted for military service because of greater physical strength and stamina. Many men today are refusing military involvement, some doubtless from a natural desire not to be maimed or killed, but more from a deep conviction that the present war in Vietnam is immoral and unjust. Some have reached the conclusion that no war with its colossal destruction can today be efficacious or just. In this judgment the sexes tend to converge today more than formerly, for women as the childbearers of the race have long been more averse to war than men.

Let us revert now to the Christian doctrine of creation, and in particular to an ongoing, continuous process of creation. Each child who is born, whichever the sex, is a part of this creation, though it by no means follows that every child ought to be born. Death is an inevitable fact in God's world, but it cannot truly be said that the time and manner of every death is the will of God. Neither can it be said that every birth, in this state of society on an overcrowded planet, is God's will. In these crucial events, as in all else in human life, there ought to be responsible human action in such spheres as are open to human initiative. Every child that comes into the world is a part of God's continuing creativity through human channels. Every child ought therefore to be well born, well nurtured in all that body and spirit require, loved and brought to the fullest and best maturity. In all this, men and women are co-creators with the Eternal.

We have noted repeatedly the complementary nature

of the sexes and the need for fellowship between men and women on a broader base than the conjugal union. The latter is vitally important and ought to take place within a marriage blessed by mutual love and fidelity, in which there is a self-giving of spirit as well as the bodily union which the Bible refers to as one flesh. Whether or not marriage is viewed ecclesiastically as a sacrament of the church, it is certainly, as the time-honored ritual says, "an honorable estate, instituted of God." Although this is not the main theme of this book, it ought in no sense to be disparaged or treated lightly. It is basic to much that is fundamental in human society.

We noted at the beginning of this chapter that a theology of sex is related to the wider structure of Christian thought at four main points: creation, the Christian understanding of Man, redemption and its mediation, and our social responsibilities. We shall turn in the next chapter to the second of these themes.

VIII What is man— and woman?

No theological understanding of the place of women in the total order of creation would be complete without a look at the Christian understanding of Man in the generic sense, and within this the dual sexuality which gives to woman a distinctive role. At many points it is a role shared with the male sex, and at no point ought it to be viewed as a subordinate one.

1. *The image of God*

In examining the biblical accounts of creation we found a basic note to be the creation of Man, male and female, in the image of God. Since love, goodness, wisdom, and creativity are found in human nature at their highest, these qualities in infinite degree may well be thought to characterize, though not to limit or define, the nature of God. Even though this approach is based on a form of analogical reasoning by which we start from the seen to try to grasp in some measure the mystery of the unseen, I believe it to be a legitimate one if adequately safeguarded. In this discussion I shall try to elaborate further the relation of Man to God, to the animal world, and to his neighbor or fellowman.

The true ontological relation is from God to Man, and not the reverse. For purposes of inquiry one may move from Man to God, but this is not the order of creation or of existence. This would not need to be emphasized except for a recurrent tendency to think and speak of Man as if he were all-sufficient, and hence as if God were made in Man's image. Yet Man is not God, not even in the sense of a "divine spark" emanating from the divine, as popular usage often assumes. It is to God that we owe our origin as human creatures, and because of this fact in conjunction with God's loving concern, we owe to him our trust, obedience, and worship.

God is the supreme Creator and Determiner of Destiny, even though Man may thwart the divine will and mar his image by ignorance, indifference, and sin. What this means in reference to our dual sexuality is more far-reaching than may appear on the surface. To look again at the Genesis stories, it is not the biological side of sex that is there accented. Man is bidden to "be fruitful and multiply," but there is no suggestion that this is humanity's only task. The divine blessing is given also for stewardship over nature and the conquest of its recalcitrant elements. Furthermore, in the Yahwist story it is as an answer to man's loneliness, not to provide him with sexual satisfaction, that woman is created.

We do not need to take the particular words of an ancient story as definitive, but they do cast light on what a comprehensive survey of the human situation indicates. We are made male and female for sexual union and the procreation of the race, but for a great deal more than that. We are created in two sexes with both bearing the divine image to do the will and the work of God in the world. When those of either sex disregard this divine origin and destiny, all sorts of evil consequences result.

These consequences appear in our time. The Bible is not squeamish about sexual union; it is regarded as good and ordained of God. But it is not treated as a physiological function to be engaged in simply for personal pleasure. There is polygamy in the Old Testament which had given way to monogamy by the time of Jesus and considerably before, but promiscuity in sex relations is repeatedly condemned. This is quite different from the mood of the present. The Kinsey reports of the 1950s approached the sexual behavior of both male and female entirely from a biological point of view, and their findings indicated that large numbers of their respondents viewed it in the same light. The more recent Masters and Johnson studies have a broader conception of sexual duality, but with the present social attitudes toward sex they are apt to be read from a prurient rather than a scientific interest. Meanwhile pornography abounds, causing much difference of opinion as to how it ought to be dealt with. The Playboy philosophy, the accenting of nudity, obscenity, and sexual perversions in the movies and drama, the extremes of flight from prudery in much current journalism and other writing, and other evidences of the breakdown of former sexual disciplines, all tend to place sex on a biological basis not far removed from the animal world. Sexual union ought to be viewed as a natural function with a high social and spiritual meaning; we seem not to be moving in this direction.

But, as has previously been indicated, sex in this sense is not our main theme. The main concern of this book is the equality of women as persons. The subordination of women as if they were inferior beings, and the resultant reduction of the status of women to that of adjuncts to men, whether sexually, domestically, or professionally, are a denial of the basic equality of the sexes as made in the image of God. To close the doors to opportunities for service in public life is to raise barriers to much that we may well believe God desires women to be doing. Even though this point of view in deference to a long past is accepted and accented in the churches, this does not make it right in the sight of God.

But the other side of the matter is also related to the divine image. To rebel against being a woman and try to be mannish in all one's ways is also to deny one's birthright and destiny. There is a parallel here with the racial situation. For many years the Negro was made to feel inferior until he came to regard himself as such, and those who rebelled against this status tried to imitate and emulate white persons. Now, the mood is to be proud of one's color because "black is beautiful." Though there are excesses in both white racism and black racism, this is a more wholesome mood. If we are able to see the divine image within differences of both sex and color, we can hope for a better society with both equality and pluralism.

To discern the divine image within us, we need to look to God in gratitude. But we need also to look toward the subhuman world. Man is more than an animal, whether in his sex life or any other part of his nature. Yet he is an animal with strong biological impulses, and these need to be reckoned with.

Man is both nature and spirit. There is no point in denying that Man, though created by God in his own likeness, is still a part of nature, largely sharing his bodily structure with the higher mammals. Fifty or seventy-five years ago, to point to Man's evolutionary development from subhuman animal life was to open oneself to the charge of heresy.[1] Fortunately, today one may believe in both God and evolution wihout causing great alarm. Man's physiological structure with its intricate combination of bones, blood, muscles, cellular

185

tissue, nerves, sense organs, and internal organs is very much like that of the higher animal, though with a more complex nervous system and often with a less acute sensory equipment and fewer instincts for guidance. Three basic drives Man shares with the subhuman animal world: hunger, self-preservation, and the sexual impulse.

Yet Man is vastly more than an animal in the usual meaning of that term. It is Man's spirit that makes the difference, and it is this which constitutes the divine image within him. This may be variously defined as Man's essential differences from the animal world: his vastly greater capacity for loving and for reasoning, his educability and the power to learn from the accumulated wisdom of the race, his ability to project goals into the future and to pursue them at great personal cost, his freedom to act responsibly and feel the prompting or the sting of conscience, his power to create and use language for communication, his artistic sensibilities and vast achievements in this field, even his power to laugh, and to laugh at himself as well at other objects. All this together is sometimes summed up as Man's power of self-transcendence and of self-determination. These terms are appropriate but, unless qualified, somewhat misleading, for, as we shall note further in the next section, Man never completely transcends himself or determines fully the course his life will take.

Man shares the three basic drives mentioned above with the animal kingdom. But the human spirit enables him to transcend all of these while still retaining them. Hunger will drive a person to desperate ends to secure food for himself or for his family, but seldom to cannibalism. Self-preservation will normally prompt even the most sluggish person to fight to the last ounce of strength when his life is endangered. Parodoxically, this is interrupted by opposite forces sometimes indistinguishable —either by the loss of self-transcendence in suicide or its highest fulfillment in a voluntary self-offering to save another. Sexual intercourse is a biological function in both Man and beast, but Man sinks below the animal level if it is not more than that in human experience, since in the animal world there is no freely chosen responsibility or sin.

Thus far we have been speaking of generic Man. What of woman? It should be obvious that woman shares with man both nature and spirit. There is not one of the distinguishing characteristics of the human spirit that a woman does not possess. Trace them through—love, reasoning, educability, goals and their pursuit, responsible freedom, conscience, language and communication, artistic appreciations and skills, laughter—all these are as fully present in the female as in the male sex unless their exercise has been stifled through social pressures. Women have the three basic drives mentioned as well as men. Men are sometimes said to have all of them, in particular the sex impulse, more strongly than women. I am inclined to think that there are greater variations among individuals of either sex than between men and women as groups.

If what has been stated thus far is generally accepted, we come back to where we were in the preceding chapter. Women are very much like men from the standpoint of ontological nature. Yet at one very crucial point women are different; women bear children while men father them. The deduction from this fact in the context of Christian theology is clear: God intends women to continue to be the partners of men in the propagation of the race. But it is a far cry from this deduction to say that this is the *only* function a woman has, or that *all* women ought to bear children, or that a childbearing woman ought to continue on in this pursuit beyond reasonable limits of her own strength, of the family's economic situation, or the well-being of the children already born and needing the family's care and resources.

We shall look now at a third aspect of the divine image, its manward relationship, bearing in mind that Man is neither God nor beast, neither divine nor normally bestial in his relations with his fellowmen. About a "lost image" we shall speak in the next section. What human nature ought to be is indicated by a high destiny as created in the divine image. What human nature *is* does not suggest that this image has vanished, but from the standpoint of observation it is discerned most clearly in Man's relations to his fellowmen.

D. S. Bailey draws a significant contrast between the positions of Barth and Brunner as to whether the divine image is essentially sexual or has a broader base. He says, "Barth . . . maintains that the relational image of God in its Manward aspect is specifically and exclusively sexual, and consists in the general relationship of man and woman. Brunner, on the other hand, finds the image in every responsible I-Thou relation, and criticizes Barth's view on the ground that sexual polarity is not itself 'the distinctive element in Man which distinguishes him from all other creatures,' but is only 'one strand in this element.' " [2] The practical deductions drawn from Barth's position are not spelled out here, but it is evident from other sources that Barth takes "the general relationship of man and woman" to be a divinely ordained subordination of women to men—in short, a Pauline point of view read back into Genesis 1:27.[3] Bailey favors Brunner's position, as do I, and with Brunner he draws the conclusion that since God is love, his image must be expressed among human relations in terms of love. This connotes love between the sexes, but love also on a wider scale. Human destiny therefore becomes in its fullest and highest expression a "fellowship in love." [4]

I doubt that we can express it better. The relationship between the sexes, whether in sexual union, in other aspects of the marriage relation, or in the total meeting of male and female in church and in society, ought by God's design to be a fellowship in love. Where it fails to be, it deviates from God's intended destiny for mankind.

But what is love? The term is in continuous use yet seldom defined. When looked at carefully, it may mean the *agape* of self-giving without demanding a return, or the *philia* of friendship and mutual sharing, or the *eros* of romantic love. All have their place in the Christian outlook. They meet in the emotion of caring for one another and its result in action. "To be tenderly regardful and whole-heartedly involved in the needs of another is love." [5] Love is not of necessity an intense emotion; it can take the form of a persistent good will. But it is the most costing and at the same time the most productive force in the world. In genuine love both the one who gives and the one who receives are lifted to new levels of creativity. Love generates character, and with it such qualities of character as kindness, sensitivity to the needs and feelings of others, patience, persistence under strain, cooperativeness, generosity, and courage. Without it a family collapses, and without it no society can function effectively. It is in love, beyond all else, that a person is most fully human and at the same time most fully mirrors the nature of God.

I have no desire to disparage the capacity of the male sex in "the art of loving." It has been repeatedly demonstrated. Yet it is often said that the most distinctive traits of women are tenderness and an intuitive insight into the feelings and needs of others. Immediately following the definition of love which was quoted above, Ashley Montagu says, "And that is what women, when they are not confused and rendered over-anxious or turned into social workers in their own homes, have given or attempted to give their children." It may be that such maternal love tends to reach outward in empathy more than does the forcefulness of the male. In any case, women are indispensable in the creation in society of a "fellowship in love."

2. Freedom and responsibility

Neither men nor women could be creative, loving, or moral in any meaningful sense without some freedom of choice and decision. The newborn infant has none of these capacities and is tenderly cared for or neglected at the will of others. Human infancy and the period of growth to maturity is the longest of any, and during this period the child is being shaped toward making his potential freedom actual. In this development the mother has a large part, though she is by no means the only influence on the young life. Where the family relation is at its best, the father helps in love and family fellowship to guide the child forward.

We indicated earlier how greatly social influences tend toward the differentiation of male and female characteristics. Some would say that this is as *all* decisions in adult life are molded. From this it is a short step to the conclusion that Man really has no freedom of will or choice, but that even one's thoughts are the product of one's initial heredity, environment, and past experience.

This deterministic view formerly dominated the thought of the behavioral sciences, and since causal connections are so readily traceable, a defender of freedom of choice on the basis of either common sense or the Christian tradition could easily be pushed into a corner. But this determinism fails to account for a very important matter—human responsibility. If one cannot think or feel or do other than he does, the human organism becomes an intricate machine with no responsibility of its own. Knowledge of causal connections is very helpful in the effort to remedy bad situations, but why should a machine wish to make changes for the better? And how could it judge one course of action to be better than another? Or feel remorse or satisfaction at the outcome?

Because a thoroughgoing determinism cuts the ground from under both reasoned thinking and the human quest for values, whether in morality, beauty, or a sensitive and enlightened love, it is defended today less often than formerly. The causal sequences are observed for the help they afford in shaping human behavior, but among psychologists and sociologists there is less denial of the capacity of the human spirit for responsible action in the light of ideals and freely chosen goals.

In fact, we hear much today of freedom in the sense of independent action and freedom from control by others in the social milieu. Some of this is very good, and in keeping with the inalienable right to life, liberty, and the pursuit of happiness. At other points such freedom is undisciplined and often accompanied by anger and ill will toward those with whom we disagree without trying to understand what lies back of their thinking and behavior. At this point psychological and social freedom become strangely and not always fruit-fully blended. Examples are seen in the gap between parents and their adolescent sons and daughters, be-tween these same young people and the Establishment, between the races, between the nations, between those of differing economic classes or political parties. The list could be greatly extended and obviously includes both the sexes and the churches.

Women like men are endowed by God with responsi-ble freedom of choice and will. However much restricted by social pressures and in need of liberation from long-standing forces of male dominance, moral freedom is the endowment of women as fully as of men. But with free-dom come responsibilities, and these responsibilities in either sex narrow the field of open choices.

Granted the need of population control, if women concertedly stopped bearing children—a most unlikely possibility—the human race in two or three generations would come to an end. I do not propose to add this to nuclear and ecological destruction as something to worry about, but only to suggest the necessity that children continue to be born. In the bearing and rearing of chil-dren there is a legitimate freedom, but also much in-convenience and inevitable restriction. It is a price women pay for being women, and a privilege not lightly to be cast aside.

Men have long had greater social freedom, but with this freedom also come restrictions that blend with re-sponsibilities. It is still as true as when Genesis 2:18

192

was written that "it is not good that the man should be alone"; and unless a man is willing to forego marriage, it is still true in most cases that he has a family to support. With this situation, as with women, there is a legitimate freedom but also inconvenience and inevitable restriction. It is not strange, therefore, that men and women need each other as helpers and as companions in a fellowship of love. While this is most clearly evident in the family, it extends to the entire range of human relations.

We hear much today of the liberation of women, but what of the liberation of men? Paradoxically, men for centuries have kept women in subordinate positions and have thereby become chained by their own prejudices. Furthermore, men with all their freedoms tend to be more stereotyped in their patterns of living. Dr. Mary Calderone, director of SEICUS (Sex Education and Information Council of the U.S.) points this out in a significant article in *Life* entitled, "It's really the men who need liberating." Regretting a division in the attitudes of the sexes at a time when unity is greatly needed in our world, she points to the need of men to emerge "from their age-old stereotyped grooves of earning, governing and fighting, and from their compulsively fixed patterns of masculinity in dressing, professions, recreation and life-style." More important, however, is the fact that certain adjectives usually termed "feminine," such as tender, gentle, empathetic, nurturing, artistic, ought by no means to be regarded as the sole prerogatives of women. She ends her wise statement with the words, "The obligation is on us, as women, to ease the way for men to those deeper levels of relationships where power is powerless and the truest satisfactions as human beings are to be found." [6]

3. *Sinners all*

Men and women are made in the divine image; men and women jointly have both freedom and many responsibilities. One wishes that in the analysis of human nature it were not necessary to take the third step: both men and women are sinners. Paul restated the truth of the fourteenth psalm, "None is righteous, no, not one" (Rom. 3:9; Ps. 14:3).

We do not hear a great deal about sin in our time. One may speak of bad attitudes, or wrongdoing, or antisocial conduct, or of being offenders in one sphere or another, but there is little talk of sin. Psychiatrists deal with many persons in the throes of guilt or remorse, but what has caused these feelings is seldom designated as sin.

There is a reason for this avoidance of the term, and in part a sound reason. Sin is a religious category. It means defiance of or disobedience to the will of God. If God is not taken seriously, as is largely the case in a secular society, there is no point in talking about sin. Furthermore, the psychiatrist or the sociologist operates as a scientist rather than as a theologian or moralist, and sin lies outside scientific categories.

Yet sin remains a very deep-seated infection of human nature. There are sinful acts and attitudes, sins of overt action and of complacency and indifference. We sin through wrong choices and through refusing to make choices, thus being swept along through social pressures. While every sin is that of an individual, responsible before God, there are social sins in which great masses of persons sin against other large groups of persons. Among these are racial discrimination, an irresponsible use of political or economic power, and the

194

colossal evil and destructiveness of war. If the thesis of this book is a sound one, there is sin also in sex discrimination and an irresponsible use of power by either sex.

Sin is the obverse side of a responsible exercise of the moral freedom with which God has endowed us. Animals do not sin, though they may misbehave. The normally benign forces of nature at times are terribly destructive, but nobody thinks of calling the earthquake or the hurricane sinful. Sin is the unique propensity of Man because Man is unique among all God's creatures in the power to choose and follow a course of action.

What defines a sinful course of action? It may be defined legalistically, with a vast array of dos and don'ts. This procedure has long been dominant in human society and still persists, though the tendency today is to replace it with something more flexible. Laws, whether of the State or the social code, serve a useful purpose and can probably never be dispensed with in an ordered society. However, as is emphasized repeatedly in New Testament thought, it is essential that the law be kept subordinate to the gospel of love.

Where sin is defined not legalistically but as a rebellion of the human spirit against the divine will, two principal criteria have been used through the ages. One of these identifies sin with pride, the desire to be "like God," exalting human presumption above the authority of God. Augustine was the chief progenitor of this way of thinking, with an accent on concupiscence, or insatiable desire, as that in Man which tempts him to seek his own will and way in defiance of God's. The other main criterion is the absence of love, the exaltation of self-concern above the love of God and neighbor.

This more directly accords with the recorded words and spirit of Jesus. Yet there is no sharp differentiation between pride and selfishness as sinful, for both accent self-centeredness, the exalting of the human ego above the claims of the Most High. Either approach leads to a defiance or evasion of a God-given responsibility to minister to human needs.

But what of original sin and the "lost image"? As previously indicated, the doctrine of original sin is derived primarily from Paul, for after the Genesis account of the Fall the rest of the Old Testament does not view sin as traceable to Adam or as a curse laid upon humanity through his transgression. In my judgement it is a mistake for theologians today to speak of "before" and "after" the Fall as if there were historically a time of complete primordial innocence followed by the coming of sin into the world. What needs to be emphasized is the fact of sin throughout the past, present, and presumably the human future on earth. But to literalize the myth of Adam's transgression and the Fall is to miss its meaning as pictorial language, though for some reason even theologians who have long recognized its mythological nature often continue to speak of it as if it were a historical event.

What of the relation of sexuality to sin? This is a long story and a large issue, but a few main points can be touched upon as a basis for better understanding of our present situation.

Jesus, we saw, regarded and treated women as the equals of men and gave dignity and sanctity to marriage. "From the beginning of creation, 'God made them male and female.' 'For this reason a man shall leave his father and mother and be joined to his wife, and the two shall become one.' So they are no longer two but one.

What therefore God has joined together, let not man put asunder" (Mark 10:6-9). No greater words were ever spoken about the goodness and divinely ordained character of marriage. Paul approved of marriage and its sexual consummation, though with some hesitancy, and counseled the single to remain in that state because of the approaching end of the world unless their sexual desires overcame them.

However, in the period of the Church Fathers, this moderate position changed radically. Jerome and Tertullian, in particular, lashed out violently both at the sinfulness of sexual intercourse and at women as the seducers of men to engage in it. Even within marriage it was viewed as shameful and Tertullian declared that between marriage and fornication there was a legal but not an intrinsic difference.[7] Both he and Jerome readily connected sexual temptation with the fall of Man, though like most of the Church Fathers they gave a grudging recognition to the need of marriage for the propagation of the race. And along with this attack on the sexual act itself, there were vehement attacks on women as the tempters of men from Eve onward. There were injunctions against cosmetics and every kind of adornment on the ground that they might excite lust in the beholder, and "even natural beauty," said Tertullian, "ought to be obliterated by concealment and neglect, since it is dangerous to those who look upon it."[8] In church the woman must be veiled, not just because Paul said so, but because by uncovering her face she might tempt another to sin.

Tertullian's invective comes to a climax in these words:

Do you not know that each of you is also an Eve? . . . You are the devil's gateway, you are the unsealer of that forbidden tree, you are the first deserter of the divine law, you are the one who persuaded him whom the devil was too weak to attack. How easily you destroyed man, the image of God! Because of the death which you brought upon us, even the Son of God had to die! [9]

Obviously, the scenario was being prepared for the celibacy of the clergy and an ecclesiastical sanction of the inferiority of women.

Augustine had a somewhat higher appreciation of the marriage bond, though he viewed it as existing principally for the procreation of children and as a lower state than celibacy. His own conversion was so closely connected with the conquest of sexual desire that he could never quite dissociate this from sin. Concupiscence was an insatiable desire of any kind, but among all human desires the sexual was the most likely to pull men away from God. To engage in sexual intercourse for pleasure rather than procreation was a venial sin. This position led Augustine to a virtual equating of original sin, concupiscence, and the emotions present in intercourse. His conclusion was that while in theory coitus is good because ordained of God, in practice as used by fallen Man it is intrinsically evil. Every child, therefore, is literally conceived in sin. In view of Augustine's influence in subsequent Christian history, he "must bear no small responsibility for the insinuation into our culture of the idea, still widely current, that Christianity regards sexuality as something peculiarly tainted with evil." [10]

Thomas Aquinas in general followed Augustine's interpretation of sex but with somewhat less suspicion of bodily pleasure. However, a new note appears in the attribution of sinfulness to sex. That is good which is

rational; that is evil which obstructs rationality. Therefore, since sexual experience is essentially prompted by
and experienced in a powerful emotion, virginity is to
be preferred to marriage. Two notes are interwoven
without full consistency in his thought: Since God
created Man's bodily nature with sexual functions for
propagation, coitus is good when performed by married
persons in a state of grace, but because of the Fall it is
infected with a taint of evil.

What of Protestantism? Did its founders carry along
the idea that the Fall had tainted sexuality with sin?
The answer must be both Yes and No. As is well known,
both Luther and Calvin rejected the idea that virginity
is a higher state than marriage, and with it the celibacy
of the clergy, and both men demonstrated this rejection
by marrying. But this does not mean that they gave up
all formerly held ideas on the matter.

Luther regarded wedlock as God's gift to mankind
for the preservation of chastity against an otherwise
insatiable impulse derived from the original transgression of Adam and Eve. This was its theological justification, though he did not deny that other satisfactions, as
well as trials, are to be found in family life. He did not
want marriage to become a sensual pigsty, yet it still
remained tainted with residual evil. He retained much
of the Roman Catholic rigidity in regard to divorce,
even to preferring Philip of Hesse's bigamy to divorce
when no adultery could be charged against the living
first wife.

Marriage, for Calvin, was a high calling, and he held
that it was effrontery to brand as unclean what Christ
had honored. As a consequence he was very stern in his
condemnation of adultery, and while he did not go so
far as to say that the adulterer should be stoned, he

justified the Deuteronomic provision for this penalty.[11] This may explain "the scarlet letter" in New England Puritanism. Calvin's views on marriage were a mixture of a number of positions. There are hints in his writing that woman was created not merely to be the companion of man's bedchamber but of his whole life.[12] This took on a prudential turn as he stated his own desire for a wife who "affords me some hope that she will be solicitous for my personal health and prosperity." But again he stated the purpose of marriage in blunt terms not unrelated to the views of his predecessors. "For what else is marriage than the union of male and female? Why, indeed, was it instituted except for these two ends, either to beget offspring or as a remedy for incontinence?" [13]

I have included this survey of theological attitudes toward sexuality and marriage for two principal reasons. One of these is to illustrate the damage done over the centuries by reading too literally the story of the Fall. It has led some of the wisest and greatest, most honored and influential of theologians to view the sexual relation with suspicion, and has cast a dark shadow over what ought to be a holy relationship undergirded with love. In Roman Catholicism, the celibacy of the priesthood and opposition to birth control are directly related to it.

A second reason for the survey is to point out that Eve, as the progenitor of the female half of humanity, has been stigmatized as the author of sin. This has again and again led to the viewing of women, not as companions or even as "helpmeets" to men except in a pejorative sense, but as the betrayers and seducers of the male sex. The double standard in sexual morals which has put the penalty for infractions primarily on the woman is related not only to the overt fact of her pregnancy but to a social stigma from a long past. But that this is a true description of the status of women because a serpent in a garden long ago beguiled a woman to beguile a man into disobedience—this I must deny with whatever vigor God affords me!

Yet the divine image remains, freedom remains, sin remains. Together they make of human nature—both male and female human nature—what Pascal called "the grandeur and the wretchedness of man."

4. *The forward look*

I do not wish to leave this chapter with sin as the last word about the nature of Man, whether male or female. It is never God's last word, nor should it be ours.

Basic to the Christian understanding of Man is the belief that life can be radically changed. The oft-repeated saying, "You can't change human nature," has some truth in it, but it is at best a half-truth, and as commonly spoken it is too pessimistic an outlook. Man's inborn equipment varies little from age to age, and while such variations as come in the order of nature can be influenced somewhat by eugenics and healthier bodily conditions, the biologically grounded elements in human nature are largely unchanged. Yet vast changes in the human spirit can take place and are continually being wrought. This is basically what civilization means, and why a civilization collapses when the changes are in an adverse direction.

Are we today going ahead or backward? A glance at the present scene, especially in America, shows a great deal of turmoil and unrest, of doubt and despair, and a lack of a hopeful forward look. Old standards of morality have in many cases broken loose from their moorings, and new ones have not yet been stabilized. There is fear of nuclear or ecological destruction and talk of the decay if not the annihilation of mankind. But there is also kindness, and there is conscience. A deepening of religious concern is underneath some rejection of the churches, and within the churches a lively renewal in both worship and service to the world. Among many people, especially the younger generation, along with elements of the bizarre in life-styles there is also a fresh quest for enduring values under the motivation of a more loving concern for the victims of injustice. Human nature in our day is in process of undergoing changes of great moment to mankind. It is a time of difficulty and struggle, but it is no time to yield to discouragement.

In the individual, the malleability of human nature lies at the foundation of the growth process. Without it, there would be no movement from helpless infancy to maturity. Within the person who has gradually acquired responsibility for the direction of his life, great changes in his human nature are an open possibility.

This possibility lies at the heart of the Christian doctrine of redemption. Both the burden of sin through self-centeredness and rebellion so vividly portrayed in the Bible and the inner psychological turmoil in which one often finds himself can be lifted. One finds then a new inner motivation, new sources of strength, a new outlook on the world, a new joy through the grace of God, a new capacity to go forward in confidence toward oneself and in compassion toward others.

This change is possible in the Christian because he believes, and acts upon the belief, that Christ is the supreme bearer of the grace of God. It is literally true and has many times been demonstrated in experience that "if any one is in Christ, he is a new creation" (II Cor. 5:17). It is true, that is, if to be "in Christ" is to mean a whole-souled self-giving in trust, commitment, and obedience. The term "Christian influence" is often used too superficially. The word influence in its derivation means a "flowing in." When Christ flows into a life to change its course, and one becomes Christ-directed in his thinking, his loving, and his living, he is a new person.

One fact in reference to women has almost never been questioned in the history of Christian thought: such redemption and new creation are open to women as well as to men. The leadership of women in the churches has perennially and to the present been curtailed and questioned. Yet from the beginnings of Christianity, women have been among the members of churches. This, we saw, characterized one side of Paul's attitude toward women. Women might not speak in the services of worship, and, "if there is anything they desire to know, let them ask their husbands at home" (I Cor. 14:35). Yet women had souls to be saved; women could be baptized; women could attend church services; women could open their homes for worship in the "house church." To this extent, even in their subordination, women were members of the fellowship in Christ.

It is an evidence of the power of Christian faith to soften even the most rigid prejudices that its exponents have, in the main, held that the grace of God for a transformed life is open to women as well as men, and that women belong in churches as fully as men. As a result, there are as many lay women as lay men in churches virtually everywhere, and quite often considerably more. A sharp disparity between the acceptance of women as members and as leaders in the churches is obvious throughout the centuries and today.

At the heart of process theology and of continuous creation lies what the late Alfred North Whitehead called "the tender elements in the world, which slowly and in quietness operate by love." [14] In such tender elements women have never been subordinate to men. I do not presume to say, as is often said, that women have by nature a greater degree of tenderness and sensitivity to human need than men. I am willing to settle for equality by nature and a greater increment instilled through the social process. Yet if even this be granted, it is evident that women, if given the opportunity, have a far-reaching role to play through tenderness and love both within the churches and in society as a whole. It is this role which we must consider in the next chapter.

IX The ordination and ministry of women

We come now to the most controversial question in regard to the place of women in the church and in the modern world. It is one on which persons of great influence and erudition have differences of opinion.

The term ministry has a double meaning. It can mean "the ministry." Or it can mean service in all its aspects—in other forms of professional religious work, in the volunteer activities of women in the churches, or in the services in the spirit of Christ that can be rendered in any situation or sphere of society. This is commonly referred to as the ministry of the laity. About this kind of ministry there is too much indifference, but not much controversy as to whether it ought to be engaged in. We shall be looking briefly at this ministry in the latter part of the chapter.

The term service is also ambiguous. In the sense of doing good wherever there is human need, everybody agrees that it ought to be done, however much disagreement there may be as to *how* it should be done. But let the term be used in the sense of a service of public worship, and there are many who think that only a man is qualified to conduct such a service.

1. *Why should women be ordained?*

Leaving aside for the present the ministry of women in the wider sense of doing good as a Christian duty, we shall concentrate for the greater part of this chapter on whether women should be ordained to the ministry of the church, or, in other terminology, should "receive holy orders." Along with this there is the practical question of whether a woman, even though ordained, is acceptable as a parish minister or must find some other channel of service. The two questions are related but not identical, for there are many women today with theological training and some with ordination who are nevertheless debarred by their sex from appointment as ministers of congregations.

I shall first state the reasons why I believe the answer to both questions should be affirmative. Unless there are sound reasons for the step, there would be no occasion for the denominations one after another to open their official doors to women in the ministry, or even to consider it. However, this is happening in numerous households of faith, and the issue is important enough to have prompted a number of studies by the World Council of Churches.[1] After presenting the affirmative side of the matter, I shall take up the objections.

I am not saying that every woman should be ordained, any more than that every man should be. I contend simply that sex alone should not be a barrier. A Wesleyan criterion of long standing in regard to men in the ministry takes the form of three questions, "Has he gifts? Has he grace? Does he bear fruit?" These queries may well be applied to women also. It is only the woman who is qualified by talent, by training, and by personal Christian vitality and dedication that is under consideration in the entire matter.

There are both theological and practical reasons why women should be ordained and accepted as pastors of churches. I shall deal mainly with the theological factors, for these are basic to any further consideration of the matter whether ecclesiastical or practical. The primary subjects to consider are the nature of the church and what is essential to its ministry, the weight of Scripture and tradition, and the Christian doctrines of creation and redemption.

First, then, what is the church? It is the fellowship of the followers of Christ, to which has been committed the responsibility of service and witness in carrying the gospel of Christ to the world. It is that body of persons of which Christ is the Head. This definition may be sharpened by noting what it is not. The church is a social institution with a ministry of service, but it is not simply a social institution doing various good works which might equally well be done by some other group. It is quite different from a secular club of congenial and respectable people, however much existing church groups may take on this character. The church has a unique mission and message which center in the extension of the life-giving gospel of Christ to the whole of human existence.

The church universal is a very meaningful term which conveys the thought that the church of Christ is intended by God to be universal throughout the world, unrestricted by human barriers of nationality, race, color, economic status, or culture. It is this goal which underlies Christian missions, the ecumenical movement, and the attempt in our time to transcend cultural and racial differences. While regrettably this goal has not yet been achieved in the existing churches, there is general acknowledgment that the church is intended by God to be supra-national, supra-racial, and supra-class in its essential nature. To this must be added that it is also supra-sex.

We noted at the end of the preceding chapter that the church has always been supra-sex in its membership—but not in its leadership, and least of all in its priesthood and ministry. We saw in chapter three that in the early church women were ordained as deaconesses, but not to a full equality of functions with the male diaconate. The Roman Catholic, the Eastern Orthodox, and the Anglican communions have never had women priests, and in spite of contemporary discussions among Catholics and Anglicans, a major change is not likely in the near future. Both Luther and Calvin believed that the priesthood of all believers included women, but this did not lead them to open the ministry to women. Luther believed that the exclusion was warranted by the need to preserve order and decency, and by women's inferior aptitudes.[2] Calvin held that a woman's subordinate status leaves her no scriptural authority to preach; rather, her specific ministry is that of motherhood.[3] However, some churches in their spiritual lineage have recently begun to ordain women. Elsewhere the practice is variable with greater freedom in many of the smaller sects. The Methodist Church has not been hampered by theological objections to ordination, but by practical aspects of its connectional system which seemed until recently to prevent full Annual Conference membership and therefore the assured appointment of women.

But what is the ministry, to which women have been occasionally accepted but more often denied? The ministry of the church and of Christ is a very special form of service in which a human figure, whether male or female, endeavors to proclaim the Christian message and lead the people toward greater vitality in the Christian life. It is a high and serious responsibility. The historic functions of the church, and of the ministry as its leaders, have been the preaching of the Word and the administering of the sacraments. These are, indeed, primary responsibilities of the minister but by no means the only ones. The many duties of a minister or priest include counseling in crises, comforting in sorrow, the encouragement of Christian fellowship, and that wide field of endeavor which used to be called "the cure of souls," instruction in the Christian heritage, a challenge to witness and service in many fields, and, in a quite different but very essential category, the administrative governance of the churches' structure.

These obviously are large tasks which call for dedication, and a combination of spiritual, vitality, mental acumen, and a love of persons. But are these the sole prerogatives of men? There is not one of them which a woman who is trained, intelligent, and devoted to her sacred calling cannot do. These things are not easy. She cannot do them entirely by her own strength and initiative. Neither can a man. It requires the empowerment of God and the cooperation of the congregation to do them effectively. But women have repeatedly demonstrated their capacity in these fields. Few who have been given "charges"—in the double meaning of charge as such work to do and the place to do it in—have failed in the endeavor. In fact, at the point of sympathetic understanding and counseling, women can feel an empathy with other women and with children better, in most cases, than a man.

Above I used the phrase "her sacred calling." The term, a call to the ministry, is not heard so often today as formerly. This is regrettable. Not everybody ought to be a minister, though every Christian ought to be ministering in whatever field he finds himself. But it is unfortunate to wash out the idea of a special vocation to the Christian ministry. To be sure, a call is not wholly an emotional experience, and it need not be something spectacular and dramatically soul-shaking. It requires a careful weighing of one's total situation to determine that to which God is calling, and therefore what one ought to choose as a life commitment. Yet the matter of an inner imperative which pursues one like "the hound of Heaven" ought not to be disparaged or taken lightly. Viewed in the total context of one's life, it may well be the Holy Spirit speaking. Women, like men, have felt this call to the ministry and have been willing to overcome great obstacles in order to follow it. There is a parallel here to what Peter said to the Jerusalem church when he returned from the encounter with the Gentile Cornelius, "If then God gave the same gift to them as he gave to us when we believed in the Lord Jesus Christ, who was I that I could withstand God?" (Acts 11:17).

The nature of the church and the nature of its ministry constitute the essential reason why barriers should not be interposed to the ordination of qualified women with an inner sense of vocation. But let us look at some other relevant theological factors.

There is the matter of Scripture and tradition. Both have long been cited as obstacles to a female priesthood, with the tradition of both church and society supported by certain biblical passages. These have earlier in this book been reviewed at length and need only be mentioned here. The most important of these are the Yahwist account of woman's subordination because made from Adam's rib as man's helper, the low position of women throughout the Old Testament, and the adverse words of Paul. To these it is often added that, since Jesus was a man, so must be his representatives upon earth, and since Jesus appointed no woman among the twelve disciples, there should be none in the ministry of his church. I shall deal with the last two arguments in the next section. As for the other scriptural citations, a better historical understanding explains their presence in the Bible without in the least committing us to take them as normative for all time. Furthermore, if Christian faith is to grow in relevance with the times, whatever enduring message lies underneath these Scripture passages or an ancient tradition must be adapted to the conditions of a new day.

There is a fresh insistence on the opening of ordination to women which has two main sources. One of these is undoubtedly the twentieth-century discovery of the capabilities of women in many fields, and with it the entrance of women into virtually all the major professions. The fact that the ministry of the church is the most difficult barrier to breach undoubtedly leads some to feel that it must be overcome, even as the denial of the right to vote actuated women a century ago. Nevertheless, there is a difference between women's liberation as this is commonly pursued and the quest for acceptance in the ministry. The one seeks freedom and self-fulfillment in whatever channels one may desire to pursue; the other seeks an opportunity for responsible service in what the seeker regards as her God-given calling. It is not to deny the legitimacy of much of the first to say that the second rests on a deeper and more Christ-centered foundation.

A second foundation of the movement for the ordination of women is a new appreciation of the attitude of Jesus toward women as this is disclosed in a careful reading of the Gospels. To be sure, Jesus said nothing about priesthood, and there were no clerical orders established until a considerable period after his death and

211

resurrection. Yet to Jesus, *women were persons,* as precious to God as were men—persons to be talked with, regarded as friends, healed in body and spirit, treated as important in spite of the prevailing Jewish subordination. Jesus was thus twenty centuries ahead of his times, and in the light of this part of the Scripture record the tradition of woman's inferiority, whether in the church or elsewhere, must be challenged and refocused.

As for the order of creation, we have noted that of the two creation stories in Genesis, the priestly account, later and more spiritually mature though it stands first in the Bible, makes no distinction between male and female as equally created in the image of God and given the divine blessing. This entails for women an equally high dignity and responsibility with men. It is not surprising that there are no women priests in the Old Testament, though there are prophetesses in both Testaments. The surrounding pagan cults were full of female goddesses and their priests, and the condemnation of Ishtar and temple prostitution helped to keep the religion of Israel above the level of the sexual. Yet this does not justify an assumption of the inherent inferiority of women.

It is this assumed inferiority of women, along with being placed on a pedestal by some aspects of chivalry, that dominates the scene today. It is this against which women in both church and society rebel. And it is this which primarily lies at the base of the refusal to ordain women and accept them as ministers of the gospel. Where it is replaced by a conviction of the Christian equality of the sexes, the doors open.

This is not to say that there are no differences between men and women. The difference between the XX and XY chromosomes makes a very important difference, to say nothing of what the social process has caused. But unless the differences are spiritual in nature and of such a kind as to disqualify women from conducting public worship, counseling, comforting and encouraging, teaching, creating and directing a Christian fellowship, these differences are not crucial to the problem we are discussing.

In the order of redemption, the church has never denied that both men and women are sinners, though the attribution of the sinfulness of mankind to Eve has been both affirmed and denied. Women are probably more conventionally moral than men in such matters as drunkenness, sexual offenses, and crimes of violence, but it is sentimental to say that they are less sinful. It is also a prejudiced judgment to say that they are more sinful through seductive wiles that induce men to evil. Both sexes contain many sinners and few saints.

Yet in redemption through Christ there is neither male nor female. This relates directly to the ordination of women. A study of this subject conducted by the World Council of Churches, which reports findings from the views of present-day theologians from various countries, contains this significant statement:

There are many interpretations of St. Paul's theology, but no one seems to disagree about Galatians 3:28—"There is neither male nor female; for ye are all one in Christ Jesus." Many theologians ask why this statement of St. Paul (which is much more in keeping with the spirit of Jesus and His relations with women in the Gospels), is not taken at least as seriously as the oft-quoted passages in I Corinthians and I Timothy. "Some of St. Paul's utterances about women in the particular circumstances of the day have blinded people to more important deliverances on his part, and have kept them from realizing that it is he who gives such clear expression to the principle inherent in the whole attitude of Christ to the children of His Heavenly Father. The whole spirit of the teaching of Jesus Christ is opposed to the continuance of the kind of discrimination that presently exists in the work of the Church." [4]

One of the historic terms applied to the church on the basis of both Scripture and tradition is "the New Israel." This is of particular importance from the angle of redemption. The attitude of the Old Testament and of both religion and culture in the environment of Jesus was patriarchal and paternalistic. No wonder there is still in orthodox Jewish religion a morning prayer in which the male thanks God that he was not born a woman! But Jesus introduced the seed of Christian sex equality which is at last bearing fruit. If the church is in reality "the new Israel," it will no longer cling to ancient patriarchal modes of thought and practice.

Here the matter may rest as to the theological reasons why qualified women who feel a call to the ministry should be ordained and appointed to the ministry of churches. But there are practical reasons as well.

One of these is to assert a principle. Acceptance of the principle may help to change existing patterns. Ordination ought to be an authentic personal commitment, not simply an instrument of social change. But ordination is appropriate for a theologically prepared woman even when she does not expect to make the parish ministry her lifework, provided she is dedicated to the service of Christ through some other channel. I may cite myself as an example. I was ordained a local deacon and then a local elder in the Methodist Church, though I expected to make teaching my lifework. I asked for ordination because I believed that the church should be alerted to the possibility of equal status for women, and

I believed this step might give some encouragement and perhaps help to open opportunities to women courageously serving small rural parishes as approved supplies. However, I have never asked for full Annual Conference membership, though this became possible in 1956.

The ordination of concerned and prepared women helps to challenge the present barriers of conservatism in the churches, and perhaps indirectly in other spheres. This would justify it when it is done seriously as a matter of principle, even if no question of expediency were involved. Yet there are important practical reasons today why qualified women should receive ordination and should be appointed to churches. In many areas the churches are understaffed or served by men of meager educational equipment. More than a few are closed for lack of an available minister, and, if the recent trend of male seminary graduates to enter other work than the parish ministry continues, this may increase rather than diminish. At the same time, women with adequate theological preparation and much ability are debarred because of their sex. This ought not to be.

2. Objections to the ordination of women

I shall now attempt to state the objections to women in the ministry as fully and fairly as possible, though since I do not regard any of them to be valid with reference to properly qualified women, this section is apt to seem biased to those of another opinion. Furthermore, I shall not hesitate to try to answer these objections.

The primary theological objection is the subordination of women as supported by Scripture and tradition. This is the position of more than a few who do not read literally the rib story of Genesis 2 or take the words of Paul as a proof-text, but who nevertheless believe that the subordination of women is divinely ordained. They are likely to believe that motherhood rather than any form of ministry in public life is the essential calling of women. So would I say also if only one form of service is possible. We shall come to this again later. But without denying the importance of either wifehood or motherhood, those who believe that partnership within equality is the divinely ordained order of existence will not contend that the doors to any type of vocation must be irrevocably closed.

A second theological reason, which seems to be presented less frequently in America than Europe but is apparently taken seriously by some theologians, is that, since Jesus was a man, no woman can fitly be his representative on earth. This seems to emphasize the maleness rather than the divinity and divine mission of Jesus in the Incarnation. Unless God is a male being—a common enough assumption in popular thought from the use of the pronoun "he" but not, we hope, held by any competent theologian—there is no point in contending that the ministers of Christ must be male beings because Jesus was one. We speak of the Holy Spirit also as "he," but does this connote maleness? Certainly, Jesus could not be human without a sex and his sex was male, but we are on safer ground to think of the Trinity as suprasexual.

A closely related argument is that Jesus chose no woman among the twelve disciples. This may have its background in the doctrine of apostolic succession, but the point is urged also by some Protestants and others who do not accept the historical validity of such a succession. In any case, the conditions of travel in those times and the sexual proprieties of all times seem a sufficient reason why Jesus did not choose a woman to accompany him in this intimate circle. Neither was there a Gentile among the twelve, and on a parity of argument there would need to be Jewish blood in every Christian minister.

An argument often adduced as closing the matter is that canon law is against it. This is true enough in some churches. But what is canon law except the codification of tradition? In no other sphere, political or social in other senses, is a law so immutable that it cannot be changed when the situation sufficiently requires it. This may necessitate a considerable upheaval and some delay, but it is to deny the force of Christian integrity to preserve a law inherited from the past when it becomes evident that justice and right require a change.

Most of the arguments usually adduced in the free churches[5] against the ordination and ministry of women are of a practical rather than theological nature. One hears that women's voices cannot be heard, or that women's bodies are unequal to the strain, or that women ought not to be out alone at night or in all kinds of weather. Granted the partial truth of such arguments, the fact remains that women in various forms of public life including the ministry have shown their ability to surmount such obstacles. There are microphones to amplify the voices of both men and women (though I confess to a dislike for hearing women, or men either, mumble softly). Most women who desire to enter the ministry are sturdy enough to endure its strains. One has only to read Margaret Henrichsen's *Seven Steeples*,[6] which is a fascinating account of her ministry in six rural parishes of a Maine circuit at one time with pastoral oversight of a seventh, to discover that a woman minister is not a sheltered houseplant or clinging vine.

Another objection of the same general order but with less foundation is the fear that a woman minister will use her pulpit to attract men erotically and this will break up families. I heard a well-known professor of a first-rank seminary use this argument some years ago. I asked him, "When you hear Maude Royden or Muriel Lester speak, do you feel erotically attracted?" His reply was, "That is different." He did not explain the nature of the difference.

There are two practical objections to women in the ministry which need to be taken somewhat seriously: that both men and women in the congregation often prefer a male minister and hesitate to deviate from custom, and that there may be a conflict between a married woman's duties in her home and in the church.

The conservatism of a congregation is the principal reason why ordained women with ample theological training and capability still find it difficult to secure placement in the parish ministry. Elsie Gibson reports in *When the Minister Is a Woman*,[7] that of her 270 ordained respondents only 81 were pastors of churches. Virtually all these parishes are in rural areas, and often the churches so small and financially so limited that a man would hesitate to take his family to them. In an urban situation it is sometimes possible for a woman to serve on a multiple staff as the assistant or associate minister. Mrs. Gibson reports 31 of these in addition to the 81 who have full charge of their parishes.

This difficulty of placement tends to direct women into other channels of service and is the basic reason why the guidance counselors usually advise a girl to look toward anything else rather than the ministry. But is it to be accepted as final and irrevocable? Kathleen Bliss in *The Service and Status of Women*[8] quotes an old American farmer who remarked, "We'd rather have had a man that warn't so good," and then proceeded to speak appreciatively of the woman who had been assigned to them. Repeatedly it has happened that a woman minister has been accepted reluctantly but before long has not only built up the church but has won the love of her people. It is these women who are making the strongest case for the ordination and ministry of women.

The possible conflict between a woman's duties as a mother and as a minister ought to be taken seriously, and it is usually taken into account by women who enter this field. I do not believe that for *any* sort of professional life a woman should neglect her children. But this does not close the issue. There are many able single women to whom this is not a problem. There are married women whose children are grown and away from home, but who still have many years in which to serve. There are widows, and some divorced women, without family responsibilities. Mrs. Gibson's book is so arranged as to present the possibilities in each of these types of domestic situation.

The younger married woman with children may do well to be "located" of her own will or take a leave of absence for a few years. Even such suffragists as Lucy Stone and Elizabeth Cady Stanton did this in their pursuits, and it is done in other professions unless some adequate provision can be made for child care. A fact often left out of account in raising this objection is that women of responsibility and good sense—and none other ought to try to be a minister—can be trusted to work out this problem. The record of the years appears to be that minister-mothers do not neglect their children, nor do the children of such mothers seem often to resent this relation. On the contrary, rich values are cited as ensuing from it.[9]

What of the husbands? Will the clash between the husband's and the wife's occupations cause serious conflicts? This depends on the nature of the husband's work, but more on the dispositions and capacities for adjustment of the parties concerned. The problems do not differ greatly from those that arise when a woman works outside the home in another field. If the husband is moved to another community, she may need temporarily to interrupt her work or find other channels of service, but this need not be final.

I shall end this survey by citing an objection which is both theological and practical. For many years I have been hearing that for some churches to ordain women while others do not will slow up the progress toward church union. How valid is this argument? Church *unity* in Christian fellowship and cooperative service is a far more vital movement in our time than the organic union of denominations, which hinges on so many factors that it is inevitably a slow process. In such fellowship and cooperation, whether at the level of the World Council of Churches, the local congregation, or in between, the churches which do and those which do not ordain women now work together without finding this a barrier. In plans of union the issue must be faced, not "swept under the rug," but such honest confrontation may well lead forward.

There are stirrings toward the acceptance of women in the ministry in many churches today. There are provisions allowing it in the Plan of Union of COCU (Consultation on Church Union) of nine American Churches which include the Protestant Episcopal, which has not yet taken this step as a denomination.[10] There are similar provisions in the deliberations looking toward the union of the United Church of Canada and the Anglican Church of that country. Even in the Roman Catholic Church the issue has been raised. As distinguished a Catholic theologian as Hans Küng has stated that "there are no dogmatic or biblical reasons against it," and that "the solution of the problem depends on the sociological conditions of the time and place. It is entirely a matter of cultural circumstance." [11]

If this be true, in the changing cultural circumstances of our time the barriers to the ordination and ministry of women are apt to continue to be lowered. But so thought the women ministers of a hundred years ago with glowing hopes! We must wait and see.

3. Other forms of ministry

I shall close with a much more rapid look at other forms of ministry open to women. These were glanced at toward the end of chapter five. The field is so extensive in its ramifications that it would require an entire book to do them justice. In these largely noncontroversial fields the only major theological issue is the one we have repeatedly emphasized, the subordination of women. This leads to lower pay in spite of legal specifications for equal pay for equal types of work, and to very limited opportunities for leadership positions and promotions in comparison with those of men.

First, let us look at other fields of professional Christian service open to women. Far exceeding in numbers and probably in total influence for the past century and a half is the field of foreign missions. From this field stem the first organizations of denominational women's groups, which have recruited and supported thousands of women who have gone as missionaries to virtually every corner of the non-Christian world. Their dedicated and sacrificial service, usually on small salaries and often in conditions of hardship, is of a range and depth that only the wisdom of God can properly estimate.

A service in the home field formerly equated with the work of the foreign missionary, though less extensive in outreach, is that of the deaconess. This has fallen off considerably on the American scene and is largely replaced by various forms of social work. In Germany the deaconess movement is still strong, each unit centering in a mother house usually with lifetime vows and rendering great service especially in hospitals and nursing. In Great Britain, the deaconess is the one woman worker in the church who is given official ordination in the Anglican communion.

A form of Christian service for women unique to America is that of the director of Christian education. Counselors urge this, if anything in the church, in preference to the ministry,[12] and many seminaries have special courses and award degrees in preparation for it. Women of ability and strong personality can usually find placement in this field, though less readily than formerly, and the trend now among women in the seminaries is toward securing the B.D. degree or its equivalent rather than the degree in religious education. This may indicate a shift in interest, or be due to the fact that the tenure of the Christian education director is insecure. When the financial situation of the church declines, she is usually the first member of the staff to be relinquished, and even in good times a man is often preferred. However, there is little doubt that the quality of Christian education in the American churches over the past half century has been improved materially through the services of women in this capacity.

A field for the services of women is also open on the staffs of the various denominational and ecumenical organizations for women. The opportunities here are limited by the size and range of activities of the organization, but a considerable number of these have grown to the point where they have an ample contingent of able women on the payroll. The salaries tend to be better than in most of the other church-related services open to women, but still to be lower than those of men doing work of equivalent responsibility.

There are numerous other fields in which some women are to be found. There are the religious Orders, Roman Catholic and in a few cases Protestant, where women find service and security but also restrictions against which protests have arisen. The women thus enrolled appear to be diminishing in numbers. There are a few women teaching in theological seminaries, and more in colleges, though here too their numbers are shrinking. Both men and women find placement difficult in the present oversupply of doctorates, and men are usually given the preference in women's colleges as well as in others. There are women journalists, women as chaplains in institutions, women in various forms of social work and parish work formerly done by deaconesses, and many women as church office secretaries who assist the pastor to keep the church alive and active.

Taken as an inclusive group, women constitute an impressive part of the labor force of churches in channels other than the parish ministry. Then why bother about their exclusion from the latter? Both a matter of principle and a practical situation are involved. There is no great likelihood that as the ministry is opened to women, there will be a great rush to enter it. Yet as long as sex discrimination is found in the official regulations of a denomination, a basic tenet of the Christian gospel will be violated. And as long as the social as well as official barriers remain, it will still be true that "the church is the last stronghold of male dominance."

We turn now to the voluntary organizations of church women, denominational and ecumenical. These afford to the ordinary housewife and the woman as a citizen, whether employed or not, a vast field of both service and self-education. Such organizations are found in some other countries, but they are much more influential and extensive in America than elsewhere. Their vitality varies from one congregation or location to another according to their leadership potentialities and the general situation. Yet their service in the aggregate is very great. These groups of women raise many thousands of dollars annually—if considered together, many millions—for local church expenses, for missions in both a world and a national context, for community projects and many kinds of social services. They help to create a fellowship, both social and spiritual, in the local church and on a wider sphere. Both by the outreach of service and by contacts with other groups in regional and national assemblies, they help to create a sense of belonging to a worldwide fellowship in Christ.

Furthermore, these voluntary women's organizations provide a training ground in leadership. They encourage women to speak and to act who might otherwise, through long conditioning, be too retiring to assert themselves except in the kitchen. Where the headquarters issue study books and other materials and sponsor studies in the Bible, Christian beliefs, social problems, and the various missionary areas, there is an enlargement of knowledge and vision which is of great importance. I know of nothing comparable in the men's lay groups, though happily there are fellowship and study groups in which both men and women participate.

This is not to say that there are no flaws in the voluntary women's groups. Sometimes, though I believe rarely, they may try to dominate the affairs of the church. At the opposite extreme, they are sometimes too weak to accomplish much. Their membership and sometimes their leadership tends to consist largely of older women, whether from the greater interest and loyalty of the latter in a changing world or for the practical reason that many of the younger women are employed and find their time and interest preempted. Sociability may be stressed beyond study or service. Yet in spite of shortcomings these voluntary women's groups provide both a great outlet and a great input for the women of the churches. No woman who is actively connected with one of them needs to feel the frustration and boredom—"the problem that has no name" of which Betty Friedan writes without mentioning the church[13]—which is the peril of the housewife with nothing creative to do outside her home.

There is a special category of service which combines aspects of both professional and voluntary service. It is that of the minister's wife. It is an important vocation for which she does well to secure preparation along with him in a theological seminary, though of course this cannot be mandatory. She is usually expected to assist both in her husband's work and in the women's society, or at least to show an interest and fill in graciously at many points. A woman who sees this as her vocation and delights in it can make a great contribution to the climate of the church. Yet she like other married women has a home to preside over and usually children to care for. No church ought to expect her to be an unpaid director of Christian education and general factotum, as happens too often.

I shall leave this survey with only a brief concluding word on the service of women in the priesthood of all believers—in their homes as wives and mothers, in the economic field as employed women, in civic and political relations as candidates for office, or simply as citizens concerned about the state of the world. Such women can be the servants of God not only in such time-honored fields as teaching and nursing and social work, but in business, medicine, law, and a host of other occupations. To try to describe the place of women in these manifold services would carry us far beyond the scope of this book.

All these types of service when done from a Christian motivation fall within the ministry of the laity. I wrote some years ago a book entitled, *The Church and Its Laity*,[14] and I need not say again what is written there. What needs to be emphasized here is that lay women are as much a part of the laity as are lay men.

The whole idea of the ministry of the laity, which burgeoned about fifteen years ago, seems to have receded somewhat in recent years. This I regret. But as a fresh interest in women's liberation in secular society and the ordination and ministry of women in the churches has come upon the scene, there is renewed opportunity to grasp the meaning of the priesthood of all believers. To the degree that women's liberation is able to open more and richer opportunities for service in any field, and uses methods of dignity in pressing toward such goals, I am ready to give it my blessing. Yet there are fields of responsible service to God and humanity within the churches which need greatly to be opened, and to be accented where open. It is this enterprise with foundations in Christian truth and justice which is my major concern.

In the introduction to a book on the ministry of the laity by another author I find these words which say clearly what I have tried to indicate about both clergy and laity, and about both men and women in either field. Let me quote them in conclusion:

Just as the term "laity" seems to raise a conflict between clergy and laity, so it is thought to exclude women. Nothing could be farther from the truth. Laity includes men, women, boys and girls, young men and young women. . . . The church, along with the culture of which it is too much a part, tends to fragment people into various and conflicting groups— men, women, youth, old age, married, unmarried, clergy, lay. The church needs to recover a sense of its wholeness, of being the people of God in which there is neither Jew nor Greek, neither slave nor free, neither male nor female—in other words, neither basic nor primary distinctions.[15]

This I believe with my whole mind and heart. And this is why I have written this book on women in church and society. What the future holds we cannot know. I am confident that the church will not go under in the tide of pessimism that engulfs our world. I am equally confident that the just demands of women for equality will not be silenced. It is my earnest hope that both men and women, in both church and society, may advance in the service of God and of his world.

Notes

I The next revolution

1. The statement was made by Miss Elizabeth Palmer, Executive Secretary of the World's Y.W.C.A., in an address on "Women in a New Age" at a National Seminar of the Woman's Division of the Methodist Church held at Tacoma, Wash., July 31-August 9, 1963.

2. This was particularly evident at the World Conference on Church and Society held under the auspices of the World Council of Churches at Geneva in 1966. American liberals long devoted to racial and economic justice found themselves under fire along with the conservatives.

3. See Joseph C. Hough, Jr., *Black Power and White Protestants: A Christian Response to the New Negro Pluralism* (New York: Oxford University Press, 1968). This gives a well-balanced interpretation of a development which many white people find difficult to understand.

4. These statements are excerpts from a copy of the original Social Creed, which was reprinted by the General Board of Christian Social Concerns and distributed at the First National Methodist Conference on "The Christian's Economic Responsibility in an Industrial Age," Oct. 30-Nov. 2, 1958. The reprint was dedicated to Bishop Herbert Welch, one of the original writers of the Social Creed, who was present and spoke at this Conference.

5. John Macqarrie in his chapter on "Problems of the New Morality" in *Three Issues of Ethics* (New York: Harper, 1970) gives an interesting commentary on the difference between the new morality as distorted from vulnerable foundations and the often traditional prescriptions of its theorists in concrete cases.

6. At the National Seminar of the Woman's Division of Christian Service mentioned above, it was reported, as of 1963, that all but ten nations in the U.N. gave women the right to vote.

7. *American Women:* Report of the President's Commission on the Status of Women, 1963 states on page 11 that women were earning only one in three of the A.B. and M.A. degrees and one in ten of the Ph.D.'s awarded by American institutions of higher learning, and that this represents a retreat from the 1930s, when two out of five A.B.'s and one out of seven Ph.D.'s were earned by women.

8. Betty Friedan in *The Feminine Mystique* (New York: W. W. Norton, 1963) was the first to call wide public attention to this malaise over the lack of satisfaction in the duties of

the home. She calls it "the problem that has no name." Kathleen Nyberg in *The New Eve* (Nashville: Abingdon Press, 1967) deals with the problem realistically but with more sympathy for the rewards of homemaking.

9. This disparity is due both to receiving less pay for comparable employment and to the fact that women usually work in subordinate and less well-paid positions. The Women's Bureau of the U.S. Department of Labor in 1968 showed the median annual wage for women to be $4,457; for men $7,664.

10. An account of many such groups was published in *Look* magazine, December 30, 1969, in an article entitled, "An Oppressed Majority Demands Its Rights." Further data on the movement are found in *Reader's Digest,* July, 1970; *Ladies' Home Journal,* August, 1970; *Time,* August 21, 1970; and *Life,* September 4, 1970. Many other periodicals have carried comments on the issue.

11. See *The Christian Century,* March 11, 1970, pp. 304-6 for an account of the interests and activities of NOW in a report of a Midwest conference sponsored by its Chicago chapter. Report written by Jill Floerke.

12. This is the estimate of Benson Y. Landis in *Religion in the United States* (New York: Barnes & Noble, 1965). Some other denominations have opened ordination to women more recently.

13. "UPUSA in Chicago: With All Deliberate Decency," in *The Christian Century,* July 1, 1970, p. 827. Report written by Michael Stone.

14. *Religion in Life,* XXXIX, No. 2, 261-71.

15. *The Woman's Pulpit,* January-March, 1970, p. 8.

16. Among these are Elsie Thomas Culver, *Women in the World of Religion* (Garden City, N.Y.: Doubleday, 1967); Margaret Brackenbury Crook, *Women and Religion* (Boston: Beacon Press, 1964); Mary Daly, *The Church and the Second Sex* (New York: Harper, 1968; Sarah Doely, ed., *Women's Liberation and the Church* (New York: Association Press, 1970).

II A long heritage

1. A. Maude Royden, *The Church and Women* (New York: George H. Doran Co.; London: James Clark and Co., n.d.), p. 14. Miss Royden was long a member of the staff of the London City Temple, and a notable woman preacher and writer.

2. Georgia Harkness, *The Sources of Western Morality* (New York: Scribner's, 1954; London: Skeffington and Son, 1955).

The London edition bears the title, *The Sources of Western Culture.*

3. L. T. Hobhouse, *Morals in Evolution* (New York: Rinehart & Winston, 1921), p. 159.

4. H. G. Wells, *The Outline of History,* revised one-volume edition (Garden City, N.Y.: Garden City Publishing Co., 1920, 1931), pp. 102, 160.

5. *Women in the World of Religion,* pp. 18-21.

6. *Ibid.,* pp. 42-43.

7. J. M. Powis Smith, *The Moral Life of the Hebrews* (Chicago: University of Chicago Press, 1923), pp. 15-17.

8. Quoted by A. Maude Royden, *The Church and Women,* p. 21.

9. Hagar is usually considered Abraham's concubine, since she was Sarah's slave. Yet in this period when polygamy was common, the lines were not sharply drawn. The King James version, the Revised Standard, and the New English Bible all say in Gen. 16:3 that Sarah gave her to Abraham "as a wife."

10. The conflict between human compassion and divine mandate adds a dramatic touch, but note that the story was being told by a writer in the stream of Isaac's, not Ishmael's, descendants.

11. Philip Van Ness Myers, *History as Past Ethics* (Boston: Ginn and Co., 1913), p. 242.

III Women in Christendom

1. William E. Phipps in *Was Jesus Married?* (New York: Harper, 1971), seriously challenges this traditional view.

2. At a session of the section on the Life and Work of Women in the Church at the Amsterdam Assembly of the World Council of Churches in 1948, no less a scholar than Karl Barth adduced this argument. Thereupon Professor G. D. Henderson of Scotland retorted, "On the basis of such an analogy there would need to be a Judas among every twelve ministers."

3. *The Interpreter's Dictionary of the Bible* (Nashville: Abingdon Press, 1962), Vol. K-Q, p. 190, article by B. H. Throckmorton, Jr.

4. *Ibid.,* Vol. A-D, pp. 864-65, article by D. M. Beck.

5. This is not an isolated experience. Claire Randall, Director of National Program Development for Church Women United, writes in an editorial on "Women as Church Decision-makers," *Tempo,* October 1, 1970, "The ultimate put-down which is a widely used technique for minimizing the contribution of women is the snigger or laugh. . . . And yet this happens consistently even in the highest echelons of the church."

6. The New English Bible translates it "wives," but gives "deaconesses" as an alternative reading.
7. Culver, *Women in the World of Religion*, p. 70.
8. R. Hugh Connolly, *Didascalia Apostolorum* (Oxford: Clarendon Press, 1929) , chap. IX, p. 88.
9. *Apostolic Constitutions*, Book VIII, 18, 20.
10. D. S. Bailey, *Sexual Relation in Christian Thought* (New York: Harper, 1959) , pp. 67-68.
11. Ignatius, *Letter to the Smyrnaeans*, chap. 13.
12. Pope Paul VI in 1970 made it possible for women to take church vows of perpetual virginity but with no requirement of entering a convent as nuns. This may be a reflection of the situation in the early church.
13. *Paedagogus*, Book II, chap. 11.
14. Calvin, *Opera*, xiii, 230.

IV The modern woman appears

1. Of the three most influential current books on the theme of women's liberation, Simone de Beauvoir's *The Second Sex* and Kate Millett's *Sexual Politics* are written by avowed atheists, while Betty Friedan in *The Feminine Mystique* is silent on the church or religion except to comment on their restrictive influence. This is an index of the differing climate of opinion today.
2. Eleanor Flexner, *Century of Struggle* (Cambridge: Belknap Press, Harvard University, 1959) , p. 15. The quotation is taken from *Familiar Letters of John and Abigail Adams*, Charles F. Adams, ed. (Boston: Houghton Mifflin, 1898) .
3. *Ibid.*, p. 16.
4. Quoted by Ashley Montagu in *The Natural Superiority of Women* (New York: Macmillan, 1954) , p. 25.
5. Simone de Beauvoir, *The Second Sex*, tr. and ed. by H. M. Parshley (New York: Knopf, 1957) , p. 121.
6. Willystine Goodsell, *The Education of Women* (New York: Macmillan, 1923) , pp. 17-20.
7. Emma Willard was the author of a *History of the United States, a Universal History*, and of textbooks on geography and astronomy, all of which were quite widely used in other seminaries than her own.
8. Phebe A. Hanaford, *Daughters of America* or *Women of the Century* (Augusta, Me: True and Co., 1882) , p. 524. This book is a remarkable compilation of biographical sketches of 973 eminent women of the first century of the American Republic—some of them preachers like Mrs. Hanaford herself

but also women as scientists, artists, reformers, educators, doctors, inventors, lawyers, journalists, missionaries, historians, literary figures, women in business, and much else. In all, twenty-six categories are included.

This book was in my family before I was born, and I inherited it. I doubt that many, if any, other copies are extant. It has been invaluable to me in the preparation of this chapter.

9. Hanaford, *Daughters of America*, p. 353. She refers also to a small book called "Authentic Anecdotes of American Slavery." I have found no other reference to these interesting titles and do not know whether copies are extant.

10. After the invention of the cotton gin, textile mills were established in New England. These employed women who at first worked twelve to fourteen hours a day and were poorly paid—though they received more than women teachers of that period.

11. Hanaford, *Daughters of America*, p. 356. Their names are listed as Lucretia Mott, Mary Grew, Abby Kimber, Elizabeth Neale, and Sarah Pugh from Pennsylvania; Emily Winslow, Abby Southwick, and Anne Greene Phillips of Massachusetts.

12. Inez Haynes Irwin, *Angels and Amazons: A Hundred Years of American Women* (Garden City, N. Y.: Doubleday, Doran and Co., 1933), p. 79.

13. Hanaford, *Daughters of America*, p. 358.

14. *Ibid.*, pp. 356-57.

15. See Friedan, *The Feminine Mystique*, p. 84, or Irwin, *Angels and Amazons*, pp. 84-86 for fuller statements of the items in the Declaration.

16. Leo Miller, *Woman and the Divine Republic* (Buffalo: Haas and Nauert, 1874), p. 7.

17. Aileen S. Kraditor in *The Ideas of the Woman Suffrage Movement, 1890-1920* (New York: Columbia University Press, 1965), pp. 77-86, gives an account of an amazing *Woman's Bible*, published in two volumes in 1895 and 1898 under the sponsorship of Mrs. Stanton. We shall come to this again in a later chapter.

18. Hanaford, *Daughters of America*, p. 367.

19. For example, in the *Woman's Bible* issue.

20. Hanaford, *Daughers of America*, p. 363.

21. *Ibid.*, pp. 364-65.

22. They were not twins. Angelina was born Feb. 20, Sarah Nov. 6, in 1805.

23. Culver, *Women in the World of Religion*, p. 177.

24. Irwin, *Angels and Amazons*, p. 108.

25. For a moving account of the career of Elizabeth Blackwell, see Dorothy Clarke Wilson, *Lone Woman* (New York: Little, Brown & Co., 1970).

V Advance and retreat

1. There were differences in temperament and what they regarded as propriety. The circumstances of the split are somewhat cloudy, but the fact that Lucy Stone and Mrs. Howe did not go along with the other two on easy divorce was one factor.

   Mrs. Howe is best known for her martial "Battle Hymn of the Republic," written in 1861 and still sung, but she later became a convinced pacifist and blended action for peace with her concern for woman suffrage. See Irwin, *Angels and Amazons,* p. 414.

2. Jo Ann Robinson in "Sex Discrimination and the Beloved Community" in *Fellowship,* July 1970, pp. 18-21, relates from her experiences in the freedom movement how women have been relegated to maid and stenographic services by both black and white men. She quotes Stokely Carmichael as saying, "The only position for women in SNCC is prone."

3. While this was mainly a Southern argument, some Northern former abolitionists collaborated in it, and Henry Blackwell published an essay, *What the South Can Do,* giving statistics to substantiate this argument.

4. Kraditor, *The Ideas of the Woman Suffrage Movement,* p. 5.

5. In the churches, there was more convergence in the North between the two movements than in the South, but the hope that women's votes might hasten the end of the liquor traffic undoubtedly won votes for suffrage in both areas.

6. This idea gradually grew in acceptance both by native-born middle-class voters and the foreign-born, and when New York passed its state suffrage amendment in 1917, it was the large immigrant population of New York City rather than the upstate communities that made it possible.

7. Irwin, *Angels and Amazons,* pp. 260-61 gives an interesting example. Asked whether political equality between black and white women would mean social equality, she replied that they were already equal, for both were disfranchised.

8. It is impossible to say with certainty whether Miss Anthony wrote the amendment, though it is probable. In any case, it appropriately took her name in its later stages.

9. She went on another hunger strike and was again forcibly fed. Her strike lasted three weeks, and on being sent to an alienist for examination his report stated, "This is a spirit

like Joan of Arc. . . . She will die, but she will never give up."
Public reaction brought about the sudden release of the
pickets. See Irwin, *Angels and Amazons,* pp. 380-88, for a full
account.

10. *Ibid.,* pp. 355-56.
11. Sophronisba P. Breckinridge, *Women in the Twentieth Cen-
    tury* (New York: McGraw Hill, 1933), p. 350. Appendix I of
    this book, pp. 347-50, contains the Declaration in full.
12. *Woman's Journal,* vol. 1, no. 42.
13. Irwin, *Angels and Amazons,* p. 299.
14. Breckinridge, *Women in the Twentieth Century,* pp. 188-90.
15. Elsie Gibson, *When the Minister Is a Woman* (New York:
    Holt, Rinehart & Winston, 1970), pp. xvii-xviii.
16. The World Council of Churches at its New Delhi Assembly
    in 1961 asked for a study of this matter. It was sponsored
    jointly by the Department of Faith and Order and that of
    the Cooperation of Men and Women in Church, Family, and
    Society. It was presented, but no policy adopted, at the
    Montreal Conference on Faith and Order in 1963.
17. See Mrs. Henrichsen's *Seven Steeples* (Boston: Houghton
    Mifflin, 1953; New York: Harper, 1967) for a graphic account
    of her preaching ministry to six churches and pastoral care
    of the seventh, all at the same time.
18. Calvin, *Opera,* vii, 684.
19. Mrs. Culver summarizes in Appendix III the data gathered
    by the World Council of Churches for the report mentioned
    above. Margaret Sittler Ermarth in *Adam's Fractured Rib*
    (Philadelphia: Fortress Press, 1970) chap. 4-9 gives more
    recent data.
20. Encyclical of April 10, 1963, Part I, section on Rights.
21. Williston Walker, *A History of the Christian Church* (New
    York: Scribner's, 1959; revised ed.) p. 517.

VI The Bible and the status of women

1. Historical criticism originated much earlier, with the New
   Testament studies of Strauss and Baur in the 1830s, but did
   not greatly extend to the popular level until toward the end
   of the century when heresy trials brought it to public attention.
2. Hanaford, *Daughters of America,* p. 438.
3. Kraditor, *The Ideas of the Woman Suffrage Movement,* pp.
   77-84.
4. I have followed the dating adopted by Bernhard W. Anderson
   in *Understanding the Old Testament* (Englewood Cliffs, N.J.:

Prentice-Hall, 1957). See page 383 for a chart indicating the connections among the four strands.

5. Kraditor, *The Ideas of the Woman Suffrage Movement*, p. 90.
6. B. W. Anderson *Understanding the Old Testament*, p. 386, n. 12, attributes this figure of speech to Gerhard von Rad.
7. Karl Barth, *The Doctrine of Creation; Church Dogmatics*, tr. by Harold Knight *et al.* (Edinburgh: T. & T. Clark, 1960), III/2, p. 286.
8. Quotations in Helmut Thielicke, *The Ethics of Sex*, tr. by John W. Doberstein (New York: Harper, 1964), pp. 8-9. See *Theological Dictionary of the New Testament*, ed. Gerhard Kittel (Grand Rapids, Mich.: Eerdmans, 1964), I, 781, 4.

VII Sex and continuous creation

1. D. S. Bailey, *Sexual Relation in Christian Thought* (New York: Harper, 1959).
2. Walter Marshall Horton, *Christian Theology: An Ecumenical Approach* (New York: Harper, 1955), p. 119.
3. Emil Brunner, *Man in Revolt* (Philadelphia: Westminster Press, 1947), p. 345.
4. Ashley Montagu in *The Natural Superiority of Women*, pp. 64-70, cites data which establish this fact. Among other items he states, "The biggest human brain on record was that of an idiot: one of the smallest was that of the gifted French writer Anatole France. The idiot's brain weighed over 2,850 grams; the brain of Anatole France only 1,100 grams" (p. 65).
5. *Ibid.*, p. 128.
6. Simone de Beauvoir, *The Second Sex*, p. 273.

VIII What is man—and woman?

1. The heresy trials in the seminaries were in the late nineteenth and early twentieth centuries. However, the case involving evolution which became most famous was the Scopes trial in Dayton, Tenn., in 1925, when the issue centered in the right to teach evolutionary theory in the public schools of the state. Clarence Darrow, a noted criminal lawyer, defended the young biology teacher, John Scopes, while William Jennings Bryan defended the fundamentalist religious position. The prosecution won, and the law remained on the statute books of Tennessee for many years thereafter.
2. Bailey, *Sexual Relation in Christian Thought*, p. 268.
3. *Ibid.*, pp. 293-94. In the Commission on the Life and Work of Women at the Amsterdam Assembly of the World Council of Churches in 1948, Barth denied the right of women to

positions of authority in either church or state, resting this contention on Gen. 2: 21-22 and Eph. 5:22-24.

4. Bailey, *Sexual Relation in Christian Thought*, p. 269.
5. Montagu, *The Natural Superiority of Women,* p. 145.
6. *Life* magazine, September 4, 1970, p. 24.
7. Tertullian, *De exhortatione castitatis,* ix.
8. *De cultu feminarum,* ii, 2.
9. *Ibid.,* i, 1.
10. Bailey, *Sexual Relation in Christian Thought,* p. 59.
11. Calvin, *Opera,* xxviii, 52.
12. *Opera,* i, 14. Commentary on Gen. 2:18.
13. *Opera,* xa, 231. *Advices on Matrimonial Questions.*
14. A. N. Whitehead, *Process and Reality* (London and New York: Macmillan, 1929) , p. 520.

IX The ordination and ministry of women

1. A request from the Bishops' Council of the Church of Sweden prompted such a study in 1958, and action by the New Delhi Assembly of the World Council of Churches in 1961 led to another in 1963. Under the able leadership of Miss Madeleine Barot, the Commission on the Cooperation of Men and Women in Church, Family, and Society has from time to time issued material on this and other aspects of the place of women in the churches.
2. Luther, *Werke,* xii, 375 ff.
3. Calvin, *Opera,* vii, 177, 200, 448.
4. "Report on Women in the Ministry," May, 1958, mimeographed, pp. 6-7. Quoted section is taken from a booklet, "According to the Mind of Christ," by the Rev. Prof. G. D. Henderson, published in Aberdeen, Scotland, undated, p. 6.
5. The term "free church" is ambiguous, but it seems necessary to continue to use it. As used here, it refers to those churches professing to derive their authority from a fellowship in Christ rather than an apostolic succession in the priesthood.
6. Margaret Henrichsen, *Seven Steeples* (Boston: Houghton Mifflin, 1953; New York: Harper paperback, 1967) .
7. Elsie Gibson, *When the Minister Is a Woman,* p. xvii.
8. Kathleen Bliss, *The Service and Status of Women* (London: S.C.M. Press, 1952) , p. 159.
9. Gibson, *When the Minister Is a Woman,* pp. 107-11.
10. Since 1970, women may be ordained to the diaconate but at present writing not to the priesthood.
11. Quoted in Progress Report to the House of Bishops (Episcopalian) from "The Committee to Study the Place of Women in the Church's Ministry," October, 1966, p. iii.

12. Ermarth, *Adam's Fractured Rib*, p. 9, states, *"It is significant that none of the statistical studies that classify the occupations women enter after graduation even mentions church-related work as an occupation."* Italics hers.
13. Friedan, *The Feminine Mystique*, chaps. 1, 14, *et al.*
14. *The Church and Its Laity* (Nashville: Abingdon Press, 1962).
15. Francis O. Ayres, *The Ministry of the Laity* (Philadelphia: Westminster Press, 1962), p. 21.

Index